.50

(92)

GIANT
DUMPTRUCKS

NICK BALDWIN

Warne Transport Library

First published by Frederick Warne (Publishers) Ltd 1984

© Frederick Warne (Publishers) Ltd 1984

ISBN 0 7232 3249 0

Printed in Great Britain by
BAS Printers Ltd, Over Wallop, Hampshire

Phototypeset by A.K.M. Associates (U.K.) Ltd, Southall, London

Designed by Brian Harris and Mark Slade

DUMPTRUCKS
A Technical & Historical Background

Later in this book we look at the products of most of the world's dump-truck makers during the past 30 years. In this introduction we trace the origins of the very heavy-duty tipper up to the early 1950s.

As soon as mechanical tipping gear began to oust the hand-operated variety in America around 1910, larger trucks for use in quarrying and construction began to be developed. Mechanical excavators took the place of navvies and the damage they caused led to tough steel bodies replacing timber construction. A two-ton boulder dropped from a height of only 10 cms effectively doubles

in weight on impact, so bodies and vehicles had to be extra-strong.

Tailgates became damaged during off-highway loading and dumping, so the sloping 'scow-end' came into use from around 1915. Semi-imposed dump trailers reduced the shock loads on the trucks hauling them, and for really arduous conditions crawler tractors pulled wheeled or tracked dump trailers on major projects from around 1910.

To begin with, any heavy-duty truck chassis was suitable for tipping work but in the 1920s various special trucks were developed, particularly in America, where the size and quantity of major

projects justified the expense. Republic made a very robust Model 35 for nominal loads of 5 tons (in practice dumptrucks were loaded with as much as could be squeezed aboard) that had the unusual feature for 1925 of a seven-forward-speed transmission. The CJ Hug Co (contractors) developed their own tippers with scow-ended bodies in Illinois in 1921 and soon built up a good business

ABOVE
1912 White five-ton capacity steel-bodied tipper with screw and chain mechanical body hoist.

OPPOSITE
Berliets of the mid 1960s.

3

TOP
1911 Gramm six-tonner with 50 bhp engine
body mechanically tipped by gear and chain

CENTRE
Dump semi-trailers increased a truck's load
capacity and removed some of the damage
potential from loading. This bottom dump is
hauled by a Peerless in 1916.

BOTTOM
A scow-ended dump trailer hauled by a
Knox-Martin tractor in 1915. This was a
giant of its day for 15-ton loads.

soon afterwards by Motor Rail, Aveling-Barford and others. Koehring made similar machines in America, going up to a colossal half-track dumper in 1931. Half-tracked trucks were also the speciality of Linn from 1916 to 1950 and many were used as dumptrucks.

In 1926 the American Walter firm patented a 4 × 4 tractor/trailer dumptruck in which the tipping subframe was hinged at the body but supported and tipped from the tractor. The chassis-less trailer was therefore lighter and more stable as the rear wheels moved closer to the tractor when the body tipped. The system was used by Walter and many other firms in different forms, although the bottom dump trailer with trapdoors in its floor was often preferred where the ground was really rough. All-wheel drive was found to be unnecessarily complicated and costly for most applications but has been used by some dumptrucks ever since, particularly those spending their life on earth or sand. Many of the current pivot-steer machines have 4 × 4 or 6 × 6 but of the largest rigid trucks only International offer the feature claiming that increased gradients can be climbed without damaging haul road surfaces.

The famous Euclid truck started in 1934. As a division of a crane firm Euclid had initially made tracked trailers and then in 1933 made a bottom dump semi-trailer outfit based on a Ford AA. Their Trac-Truk was the first vehicle to be designed and built from the outset as a dumptruck when it appeared in 1934. However, it was not the first dumptruck recognizable as such when compared with today's giants. That distinction goes to some of the Hugs and to the top-of-the-range Mack and International chassis equipped in 1931 to work on the Hoover/Boulder Dam projects. The largest of these were Mack AP 'Bulldogs' with seven-speed gearboxes, chain drive, 150 bhp six-cylinder gas engines and

supplying them to other firms. Their range grew in size over the next 20 years, ultimately going up to a 60-short-tons gross weight model.

Though there was much less need for such vehicles in Europe, occasional very special tippers were made, like the Scottish Halley in 1922 for working at 14,000 feet altitude in a Bolivian tin quarry. It had a six-cylinder engine with high compression cylinder heads to compensate for power loss in the rarefied air. Scammell from the late 1920s also made some ultra-tough dumpers, though most UK requirements were met by agricultural tractor conversions with dump boxes added. These dumpers were produced from 1927 by Muir-Hill and

ABOVE
Dump trailers hauled by crawler tractors were used for rough off-road work from around 1910. This Best (forerunner of Caterpillar) is shown in about 1920.

aluminium bodies able to carry roughly 20 tons. For possibly the first time the bodies had safety lips or canopies at the front to protect the driver and engine from falling rocks. Just to be on the safe side the hoods of some of the Macks were also made of boiler-plate, the radiator being at the back of the hood and therefore under the canopy. Conditions were extremely arduous, with temperatures of 110° F in the shade and one-in-four gradients. Air brakes were used for possibly the first time, and to make the vehicles visible in tunnels they were finished in fluorescent paint.

By the late 1930s dumptrucks were becoming standard lines with several American specialist truck-makers. Dart made their first in 1937 and followed it with a diesel-electric coal hauler in 1939 that could carry 80 tons split between two trailers. In Britain in 1937, Foden converted one of their tippers to work backwards to avoid the risk of falling over quarry edges when dumping. In 1939 Aveling-Barford made a shuttle dumper able to work in either direction and produced their first shuttle dump-truck eight years later.

World War II brought an enormous need for fuel and metal ores. Ever larger pits, with monstrous excavators, led to more and bigger dumptrucks. White, Kenworth, Peterbilt, Mack, Euclid, Maxi, Sterling and other American firms responded to the challenge. In addition, special rubber-tyred haul units were developed for trailer work. LeTourneau and Euclid had made these from the mid-1930s and they were joined in 1940 by Caterpillar with its first rubber-tyred tractor.

The largest rigid six-wheeler of 1942 was the Maxi, made by Six Wheels Inc of Los Angeles. It had a 25 cu yd body, walking beam rear suspension incorporating gear and chain drive (which Maxi also supplied to the last few Hugs, whose production ended in the same year). Its Waukesha diesel developed 225 bhp.

Such oversize machines were far larger than vehicles permitted on the highway and had to be proportionately stronger. As their weight and dimensions were not restricted by highway legislation they began to develop along different technical lines from normal trucks. We have already noted that a diesel engine driving a generator and electric motors was tried by Dart before the war to give variable speed without the shock torque loadings caused by conventional gear changes. RG LeTourneau was one of

the pioneers of diesel-electric construction machinery, including pivot-steer dumptrucks from the time of World War II (developed from their gear-driven two-wheel bowl scraper haulers of 1938 that steered by feeding more power to one or other wheel through multi-plate clutches). Pivot-steering, in which the truck frame is in two halves and usually hinged in two planes to allow steering and variations in wheel height, has become widespread since the 1960s but has been known for more than 40 years.

Many dumptrucks in America stuck to chain drive until about 1950. This allowed differentials to be mounted away from the rear axle(s) and so increased ground clearance and allowed larger and therefore stronger units to be incorporated, including countershafts with chain sprockets rather than potentially vulnerable half shafts in the axle. Shaft drive with final reduction gearing in the wheel hubs had been used since the 1920s on some trucks, and Euclid brought this so-called planetary drive to dumptrucks in the 1930s. Mack introduced its Planidrive axles at the end of the war and had displaced chains by 1949. Planetary axles are now almost universal on shaft-driven dumptrucks of all makes.

Electric traction was one way of getting increasing engine power to the wheels in

a cushioned manner, and another was the use of the torque converter. Invented in Sweden and Germany and perfected on heavy vehicles by Leyland in 1933, it was taken to America in 1936 by the Twin Disc Clutch Co of Racine, Wisconsin and quickly adopted by makers of construction machinery and military vehicles. Twin Disc, as their name implies, had started with multiplate friction clutches to handle growing power requirements. Torque converters, like the fluid flywheels from which they were developed, multiplied the torque of an engine and fed it to the wheels far more smoothly than a conventional clutch, thereby reducing the risk of damage to the transmission. They allowed better utilisation of conventional gearboxes by cutting down the number of ratio changes drastically. A Dart in the Mesabi Iron Ranges in 1950 had its need for gear changes reduced by 99% when fitted with torque converter.

The next step was to combine torque converters with automatic or semi-automatic epicyclic gearboxes, as had been pioneered on Daimler cars around 1930. One of the leaders in this field was the Allison aircraft components firm, which General Motors bought in 1929. As well as aero engines it made epicyclic transmissions (clusters of planetary gears that were locked to the output shaft by band brakes to give different ratios). These were proved on 1939/45 military vehicles and then applied to dumptrucks, notably by Euclid after having been acquired by General Motors in 1953. This type of transmission, but without the torque converter had been used by millions of motorists on Model T Fords. Shifts could be made with power still being transmitted to the wheels so that traction and headway was not lost. This was the origin of so-called 'powershift',

LEFT
Contemporary with the first Mack dump-trucks was the International of 1931 used on the Boulder Dam construction. Bodies by that time had guards for cabs and operators.

BELOW
The first vehicle to be designed from the outset as a complete dumptruck was the Euclid Trac-Truk of 1934. It had shaft drive and I-section steel girders for the chassis.

which became a vital factor in dumptruck design.

So, many of the features that go into modern dumptrucks were in use or on the drawing boards by the early 1950s. Even the oil/air cylinders to provide low maintenance, energy-absorbing suspension had been used on some trucks and coaches before World War II. However,

The Hoover Dam Mack fleet had risen to 20 by 1933 and included AC-6 'Bulldogs' on pneumatic tyres able to carry approximately 20 tons.

disc brakes had only just been discovered and did not spread to dumptrucks for another 20 years (albeit well ahead of their tentative application to highway trucks). The need for massive and reliable engines led Euclid around 1950 to try twin power units in its largest trucks to reach an aggregate 600 bhp, although this level of power was soon available in more practical single engines and has since been doubled and trebled. Gas turbines were also tried from 1952, but found to have few advantages over diesels.

The main trend over the past 30 years has been the growth of the dumptruck industry outside its American homeland. Aveling-Barford, Foden and AEC all made quarry and construction trucks from the late 1940s. In Germany, Faun developed a twenty-tonner in 1950, and rival vehicles were soon made by Krupp and Kaelble. The Japanese construction machinery firm Komatsu made a fifteen-tonner in 1951, and the Eastern Bloc

SHULER AXLES FOR LINN TRACTORS

began to produce giant trucks to exploit their mineral resources soon afterwards.

Euclid opened its first overseas plant in Scotland in 1950, and since then the whole industry has boomed and attracted dozens of new manufacturers. Indeed, in the 1960s and 1970s dumptrucks were one of the few branches of the motor business to show sustained growth. Many of the new makes have concentrated on pivot-steer machines and some have even equipped them with diesel-driven hydrostatic wheel motors to simplify power transmission and give smooth torque comparable to that of an electric motor.

The industry is strikingly innovative and has attracted many talented engineers and businessmen. Many of the current market sector leaders such as DJB, Volvo-BM, Heathfield, Perlini, Rimpull and Lectra Haul have started in the business within the last 20 years.

In the following pages will be found details of the main products of the vast majority of firms that have made dumptrucks in the 25 years to date. Some of the smaller pivot-steer machines are more closely related to dumpers than to trucks so only a representative selection is included, as are only some of the tractor-hauled types when most closely related to dumptrucks.

Dimensions, weights and special terms

Wherever possible, the struck capacity of bodies is quoted. Struck signifies the unheaped or inside volume of the body. One cubic yard equals 0.764 cubic metres. Most dumptrucks have scow-ended bodies, in which an upward sloping rear floor does away with the need for a tailgate. Payload is only a rough guide because most trucks are designed to be able to carry as much as can be loaded onto the body, or spotting area as it is known to designers and loader operators (the spotting height being the reach required to clear its body sides). Because dumptrucks originated in America, many firms around the world continue to register the capacity of their machines in short tons, which was the original measure. Where possible we have

attempted to differentiate between short tons, tons and metric tonnes (one short ton equals 2000 lbs or 0.907 tonnes/907 kg, whereas a long ton, as frequently quoted in Britain, equals 2240 lbs).

Driving position is quoted as normal control (conventional) or forward control (cabover).

Acknowledgements

My thanks to everyone in the industry who has been so helpful, and to Russell Jones and Nick Georgano for supplying photographs and advice.

The time-honoured 'Bulldog' Mack dump-trucks were ousted by the F range launched in 1937/8. This is an FH with front radiator, chain drive, coal body and option of Mack's first home-produced diesel (diesels had been used in European 'heavies' from as early as 1923 and were in widespread use from 1930). Diesels gained slow acceptance in some American trucks from 1932.

OPPOSITE BELOW
The 80 bhp Caterpillar-powered Hug Lugger of 1937/8 had 4 × 4 plus helper wheels as an apparent afterthought. Hug production ended in 1942, 21 years after the firm had made its first special tipper for road building.

ABOVE LEFT
Caterpillar, after years of success with tracked vehicles, added wheeled haulers in 1940. This one has an 8 cu yd Athey trailer and 80/90 bhp Caterpillar diesel.

ABOVE RIGHT
Sterling was one of several Amerian firms to make chassis for dumptrucks to boost ore and fuel production in World War II. This 1941 truck had Heil body and chain drive, and its engine and radiator were protected by a boiler-plate hood.

BELOW LEFT
Walter Tractor-Trucks changed little in appearance for 30 years from the mid-1930s and all featured 4 × 4 with separate load and power-carrying members in each axle. This 35-tonner of the late 1940s could have Waukesha gas or Cummins diesel engines of 200 to 260 bhp.

LEFT
A 1943 White advertisement showing one of the reasons for the growth in demand for special quarrying vehicles.

ABOVE
Virtually all dumptruck development took place in America, although in Japan Isuzu claim to have built this vehicle as early as 1943.

BELOW LEFT
The 1942 Maxi made by Six Wheels Inc of Los Angeles had a 225 bhp Waukesha diesel and, with a 25-cu yd body, was the largest truck of its day. Its makers later joined CCC (see alphabetical section).

BELOW RIGHT
Mack made a giant chain-drive six-wheeler in 1937 and soon applied the offset-cab feature to put the driver next to one edge of the haul road. These are the early postwar LRSW 30-tonner versions with shaft drive and planetary axles.

OPPOSITE ABOVE
In 1938 LeTourneau developed two-wheeled tractors for its scrapers in America and these were soon attached to dump trailers. This is a 1948 Tournarocker E-40 with pivot-steering and diesel-electric drive.

bumper crops IN THE MAKING

ABOVE
The local Dennis agent was asked to supply dumptrucks to the Steel Company of Wales in 1947. Dennis could not fulfill the order so they turned to Foden, who converted a Gardner-engined DG model similar to this.

BELOW
Foden soon became the major British supplier, and here we see a Gardner 112 bhp-engined production version with bulldozer blade for clearing the haul road and for stockpiling.

Working on an open cast coal site, this tipper with "Pilot" body and tipping gear, is one of a fleet of "Mammoth Majors" operated by Wilson Lovatt & Sons Ltd.

In the Billingham mine of Imperial Chemical Industries Ltd. This special tipper, fitted with "Edbro-B & E" tipping gear, carries 14 tons and works entirely underground.

One of two "Mammoth Major" Tippers with "Pilot" body and gear, used by Clayton Cawood Ltd., for the transport of slag.

One of a fleet of "Mammoth Majors" with "Pilot" body and gear operated by Sir John Jackson Ltd., working on an open cast coal site.

ABOVE
A Swedish Scania-Vabis of the late 1940s with eight-cylinder-in-line engine. The apparatus behind the cab and in front of the radiator may be an exhaust cleaner for underground working.

LEFT
AEC made heavy duty tipping versions of their familiar Mammoth Major to rival Fodens and here we see a selection of 24-tons-gross vehicles in their contemporary sales leaflet.

OPPOSITE ABOVE
In 1939 Aveling-Barford made a shuttle version of one of their largest dumpers that was able to be driven and controlled in either direction. In 1947 came a 138 bhp, 15-short-ton capacity version on three axles. Note the two steering wheels, which have duplicated controls on either side of them.

RIGHT
In an effort to use the coal that it was stripping as fuel, the NCB in Britain tried this Sentinel in 1951 — surely the only steam dumptruck ever?

FAR RIGHT
The largest dumptruck of 1950 was claimed to be this 28 cu yd Heil-bodied Sterling. It had chain drive, a 325 bhp diesel and was for a coal pit in Pennsylvania. Sterling joined White in the following year.

ABOVE
This 1950 Dart had a five-speed Fuller manual gearbox plus a Twin-Disc torque converter that effectively reduced by 99% the need to change gear when carrying 35 tons. The engine was a 350 bhp Cummins diesel.

LEFT
After its takeover by PACCAR in 1945 Kenworth became a major dumptruck maker. Here is an early example with offset cab and Timken-Detroit tandem. In 1958 Dart joined Kenworth in the PACCAR group.

BELOW LEFT
The Komatsu mining machinery firm in Japan added dumptrucks to its range in 1951. This early HD150 was for 15-tonne loads. Two years later Hino launched a rival machine with forward control and half-cab.

OPPOSITE ABOVE
The Scammell Mountaineer 4 × 4 came out in 1949 and was for a gross weight of 20 tons (later increased to 24 tons, of which roughly half was load). Various engines up to about 150 bhp were available and the special suspension arrangement made for very high off-road effectiveness.

RIGHT
Max Cline left Dart to start his own dumptruck firm in 1952. One of the first Cline trucks was the 13SP (stock pile) 13-tonner shown here, which remained in production into the 1960s.

LEFT
Several German firms began to build dump-trucks in the early 1950s, notably Faun, Krupp and Kaelble. This is a Krupp Drache 4 × 4 for 11-tonne loads with 150 bhp, four-cylinder, two-stroke diesel.

CENTRE LEFT
As the loads carried by dumptrucks grew ever larger, some self-propelled dump trailers were tried to create 'trains'. Here we see one in an American coal strip-mine.

BOTTOM LEFT AND RIGHT
The prewar diesel-electric idea was revived with great success by LeTourneau (now Wabco) and gained momentum from the 1960s when General Electric offered a range of 'electric wheels' for the largest trucks. This is a diagram and sectioned wheel from a recent Komatsu 120-tonner.

OPPOSITE ABOVE
The Scottish Euclid factory opened in 1950 and brought the latest and largest American trucks across the Atlantic. This 50-foot long giant, climbing Warwick's Westgate Hill after collecting its locally produced Eagle trailer, had a 250 bhp Rolls-Royce diesel.

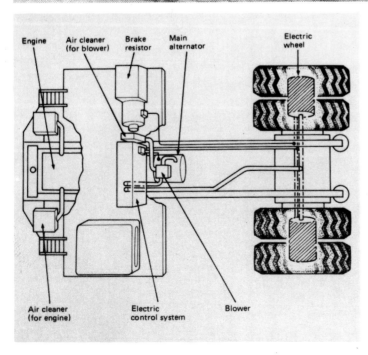

An A-Z of Major Dumptrucks produced in the Past 30 years

LEFT
With extensive knowledge of off-road vehicles gained from their acquisition of the British FWD and Hardy firms 10 years before World War II and thousands of military vehicles built during it, AEC made Heavy Duty Tippers from the late 1940s based on their Mammoth Major model (see historical introduction). These had single-spring rear bogies, double reduction rear axles and 11.3 or 9.6-litre diesels. As well as these six-wheelers, AEC also made some special trailer dump haulers using many of the same components. This mid-1950s example has an Eagle side-dump body and trailer and was tipped by an independent winch and gantry.

AEC built a massive chain-driven dumptruck prototype for Australia in the early 1950s and then in 1959 introduced into series production the giant HDK4LA Dumptruk. This was developed at their Maudslay truck factory and used the 17.75 litre AEC six-cylinder AVT 1100 diesel, developing 340 bhp (up to 410 bhp SAE gross) and a three-speed and reverse gearbox with three-stage Twin Disc torque converter using fuel drawn from the diesel tank as its hydraulic fluid. Very unusually for a truck of 46,000 lbs capacity (later uprated to 54,000 and then 60,000 lbs) it had leaf springs on the rear as well as the front axle.

About 150 were made (mostly at the Thornycroft factory acquired in 1962) with an assortment of rear and side dump bodies of 15 to 20 cu yds struck capacity.

Production had ended by the time that Aveling and Barford, with their extensive range, joined the Leyland Group in 1968 (AEC had been acquired in 1962).

The photos show one for export and four with side dump bodies on an NCB open cast coal contract.

In 1957/8 AEC replaced the Mammoth Major 6 × 4 Heavy Duty Tipper with the 7.6 m³ (10 cu yd) Dumptruk. Technically much as before, the only engine now offered was the 11.3-litre, 150 bhp A221 and a half-cab was standard. The Scottish Land Development Corporation (SLDC) were sole concessionaries on the home market.

The Dumptruk in its final Mark III form was made until 1964, when it was replaced by the 690 Dumptruk (see Aveling-Barford).

LEFT

The Italian firm Astra began by reconditioning ex-US military vehicles after World War II and evolved the first of a range of dumptrucks from these in 1955.

Shown is a 1961 Detroit 265 bhp-engined BM18 with six forward gears. A 4 × 4 model followed and a shuttle version of this with reversible controls is still in production.

CENTRE

An Astra BM35 of the late 1970s for 35,000kg loads. It has a Detroit V12 465 bhp diesel and six forward - one reverse Allison powershift transmission. Body capacity is 18.24 m^3 (23.84 cu yd) struck, and there are nitrogen/oil suspension struts both at the front and rear. The rear axle has hub reduction. Note the exhaust outlet in the body ribbing, a regular feature of many different trucks to warm the body and to stop the load from sticking.

BELOW

The famous American agricultural, industrial and construction equipment group of Allis-Chalmers, founded in 1847, briefly offered a range of pivot-steer dumptrucks in the early 1960s. This is the TR-160 for 12-ton loads with 12 cu yd body. It had a 155 bhp diesel and there was also a 230 bhp TR-260 for 20 tons. Turning radius was 23 feet and the front wheel drive incorporated a Kon-Tork limited slip differential.

Allis-Chalmers merged its construction equipment side with Fiat in the 1970s to create Fiat-Allis and the range of its products was greatly reduced.

Atkinson Vehicles Ltd, of Walton-le-Dale, Lancashire, England diversified into the special vehicle field in the late 1950s — their Omega 6 × 6 of 1957 onwards was available as a 17 cu yd dumptruck, although it is probable that none was sold. In the same year, 4 × 2 and 6 × 4 half cab, forward control 18 and 26 tons gross trucks were offered with Gardner and Cummins diesels. After a time they were known as Hy-Lode models. This is the Hy-Lode 40 (40,000 lbs capacity) with 25 cu yd coal body for use in a Scottish opencast mine. Hy-Lode production ended about 1967.

TOP

Vehicles not built specifically from the outset as dumptrucks are outside the scope of this book, but this Austin is included because it was one of a number converted by Abelsons in Birmingham. They beefed up the chassis of the previous angular-cabbed BMC and of this 1960 702, provided heavier suspension and fitted Edbro or Telehoist tipping gear and scow-ended 6 cu yd bodies. For an extremely modest £1407 complete in 1960 one had a $10\frac{1}{4}$-ton gvw dumptruck with BMC 5.1-litre 105 bhp diesel. Most went to civil engineers but one at any rate (with channel steel cab guard) spent its whole life shifting granite from face to crusher in the Laird Quarry at Malvern.

CENTRE

In 1957 the Autocar AP 40 with 600 bhp diesel was claimed to be America's largest single-engined dumptruck. It had a capacity of 40 short tons and planetary drive axles. As part of the White group, Autocar had ceased to make its range of two and three-axle giant dumptrucks by the time that Euclid joined the group in 1968, although conventional heavy-duty tippers were still produced and are still a speciality now that Euclid has been sold and White/Autocar belongs to Volvo.

BOTTOM

The SL series of Aveling-Barfords has been in continuous development since 1954 (see historical introduction for its predecessor). This is a mid-1970s example with Leyland 204 bhp six-cylinder diesel engine, five forward and three reverse gears and reversible controls. The rear axle has triple reduction and is semi-rigidly attached to the chassis via bolts with shock springs. It has a pay load of 34,000 lbs. The special exhaust purifier enabled it to work underground without causing fumes or igniting gas, and consisted of weirs immersed in an aqueous solution of soda ash and a tray of porcelain Lessing rings.

TOP

A 1971 Autocar heavy-duty, on/off highway dumptruck. Note the massive air-cleaner and cab-top air conditioner. This type of vehicle was one of Autocar's specialities and it led to the current Construcktor range of chassis. The Construcktor first appeared in 1975 and featured galvanized steel cab panels, radiator guard, full length door hinges, straight chassis rails with bolted assembly and Caterpillar, Cummins or Detroit diesels of 230 to 450 bhp. Front axle ratings went up to 20,000 lbs and tandems to 65,000 lbs.

CENTRE

In 1958 Aveling-Barford introduced the American inspired SN dumptruck with 400 bhp 16,222 cc Rolls-Royce turbo-charged eight-cylinder diesel and six forward speed constant mesh gearbox. It was for 27-ton loads but this was later increased to 30 and 35 tons. Six-cylinder Cummins and Rolls-Royce engines and torque converter/power shift transmission were also offered at the outset and later the straight-eight Rolls-Royce diesel was uprated to 450 bhp and a 476 bhp Detroit V12 made available. The SN had shock-bolt mounted planetary rear axle, a 30-foot turning radius, a 9-second dumping cycle, exhaust-heated body and 33 mph top speed. 54 were used on the Aswan Dam project after Russian equipment failed.

BOTTOM

The SN range gave way to the Centaurs in 1970 with load ratings of 22-40 tons, later increased to 50 tons. Various engines by Caterpillar, Detroit and Cummins have been offered, of 280-635 bhp, and mechanical or Allison powershift transmission are used. All have front and rear suspension cylinders filled with nitrogen and oil and have hub reduction rear axles. A 25-ton capacity Centaur 25 is shown, and later versions of both these Centaurs and the SLs are now known as RDs, this becoming the RD 025.

TOP

The 690 Dumptruk with AV690 200 bhp diesel and five-speed constant mesh gearbox that replaced its forward control predecessor at AEC in 1964 was made for a time by Thornycroft and then by Aveling-Barford from 1970, following the latter's acquisition by Leyland two years earlier. It was then transferred to the Scammell factory where it was built as the LD55 Bush Tractor and then from 1978 as an LD55 Mk II dumptruck. In its final form it had an L12 Leyland 202 bhp diesel and Fuller 5 or 6-speed gearbox. Off-road payload was 18.3 tons.

CENTRE

Bedford are one of the few volume truck producers to offer standard 4 × 4 trucks, and several of these are used in the construction industry. They do not build heavy-duty dumptrucks, although these can be built to special orders by Reynolds Boughton. The recent example shown has a 6 × 6 conversion and new chassis. Other components are from the K series Bedford. In 1965 Bedford briefly offered a special 26,000 lb gvw 4 × 2 site vehicle.

BOTTOM

Berliet unveiled their remarkable 100-tonne gross weight T100 truck in 1957. It had a V12, 30-litre, Cummins 600 bhp diesel and four-speed manual gearbox with two-speed transfer box and air-actuated clutch. The chassis was intended primarily for oilfield work and cost £55,000. Only a handful of the behemoths were sold.

ABOVE
BelAZ in Russia started making giant dump-trucks in 1959, and this is a 1964 example for 65-ton loads with 375 bhp, V12 diesel, torque converter transmission and air/hydraulic suspension. More usually it was seen in two-axle 30-tonnes capacity form and updated versions are still in production. The engine was reputedly developed for military vehicles and many have been replaced by Polish Wola H units. Larger models of 660, 880 and 1695 kw (900, 1200 and 2305 bhp) have since 1978 been fitted with French SEMT Pielstick engines (180 in 1981 alone), and some have electric drive. The BelAZ name is also applied to KrAZ dumptrucks sold in certain countries, including Britain.

CENTRE
Dumptrucks are vital to China's industrial plans and at present most are imported. But some are made in China such as Beijing (see also Shanghai and Jiefang). The Beijing for 20-tonne loads first appeared in 1977 with locally produced Santong engine, but this was not successful, so since 1981 Polish Wola or American Caterpillar and Detroit diesels of up to 245 bhp have been specified.

LEFT
In 1964 Berliet tried to break into the new pivot-steer market with the T-40 for 40-tonne loads. It was an experimental vehicle with diesel-electric drive and LeTourneau motors in all four wheel hubs. Once on the move, drive gradually switched to the front wheels alone, and top speed was 37 mph. At the same time the conventional half-cab, two axle rigid T-18 and T-25 with 240 and 320 bhp engines and manual five-speed gearboxes made rather more impact.

ABOVE LEFT
The famous snub-nosed Berliets had been around for some 20 years when this G series 10m³ (13 cu yd) dumptruck version was exported to China in 1967. It is believed to have been powered by a 180 bhp Berliet diesel, although other models in the series had 200, 240 and 320 bhp diesels.

Berliet and their associate company in Algeria received an order from Red China in 1965 for 1035 assorted heavy trucks and this was followed in 1967 by an order for 100 dumptrucks like these and 500 6 × 4 heavy haulage tractors. China acquired a licence to produce these models and it is believed that some may still be in production there.

ABOVE RIGHT
The Soc des Bennes Brimont of Rethel in France have made pivot-steer dumptrucks since the mid-1960s. This is a 1968 BB9 for 17-tonne loads (28 tonnes gross). It had a capacity of 11m³, 180° frame articulation and a Unic 125 bhp diesel.

In 1974 Brimont added the Latil 4 × 4 chassis to its range, and some of these have been built as site tippers.

LEFT
In 1968 Berliet received an order for 30 T-60 trucks for a diamond mine at Omsk in Siberia. They were similar to the ones on the production line here and had Cummins V12 634 bhp diesels and six-speed Allison fully automatic transmission with splitters. To cope with temperatures as low as –60°C they had fully enclosed and insulated engines, heating elements on many components, a radiator that could be blanked off completely, heated batteries and an exhaust purifier for underground work.

In 1974 Berliet came under Renault control and the giant specifically dumptruck models were discontinued, although versions of the heavy duty G range of bonneted trucks continued to be offered.

One thinks of Büssing trucks as all having underfloor engines which would plainly not suit arduous off-road work where good ground clearance was critical. However, when they built this LS 11F/16 in 1958 they offered both this variety of in-cab engine and also a normal control/conventional version. The diesel developed 185 bhp SAE and payload was 7650kg (16,870 lbs) or more when working off-highway. Bodies and tipping gear were by Meiller. Büssing was taken over by MAN in 1971 and subsequently made only underfloor-engined road vehicles.

BELOW
In 1962 Caterpillar entered the rigid dump-truck field with the 769 for loads of 35 short tons (31.8 tonnes). It had a 309 kW (415 bhp gross) Caterpillar six-cylinder 14.6-litre diesel and three-range, three-speed planetary power shift transmission with a single lever. In each of the three main ratios a speed sensor automatically up-shifted through its three ranges before the lever had to be moved to the next ratio. Suspension was by oil/air cylinders at each wheel and the brakes on the back wheels were of the oil-cooled disc type. The model is still in production, having been updated several times over the years.

RIGHT
As its name implies, the Crane Carrier Corporation of Tulsa, Oklahoma, started by making chassis for mobile cranes. It branched into other fields of construction vehicle manufacture and took over the Available and Maxi truck firms by the late 1950s. For a time CCC competed in this field before concentrating on refuse, crane and mixer chassis from the 1970s. Their quarry and construction vehicles of the early 1960s included both dumpers with reversible controls and dumptrucks, like the LCM450 shown here. In the mid 1960s a normal control/conventional CCC dumptruck was made in the company's Australian factory and a series of conventional six wheel heavy duty tippers was also made in America in 1977 mainly for the Middle East.

CENTRE
An interesting prototype in 1966 was the Caterpillar 783 with Caterpillar V12 1000 bhp turbocharged diesel, disc brakes and steering on both the front and rear axles. It had a 100-ton capacity side tipping body with automatically opening sidewall. In fact it did not go into production and instead Caterpillar made even larger two-axle models which now go up to 85 short tons (77 tonnes) capacity and articulated trailer hauling version of most for up to 150-ton loads with 650 kW (870 bhp gross) diesels.

BELOW
The Caterpillar 773B (1978 example shown) is for loads of 45.4 tonnes (50 short tons) and has oil-cooled disc brakes, oleo-pneumatic suspension, seven forward ratio Caterpillar automatic transmission and Caterpillar V12, 27-litre, 485 kW (650 bhp) diesel with planetary reduction rear axle. The truck is 29ft 11in long, 13ft 4in high and 13ft 4in wide and the body struck capacity is 26 m³ (34 cu yds). Total loaded weight is 83.3 tonnes (183,645 lbs). Top speed is 61 km/h (38mph).

OPPOSITE ABOVE
Max Cline worked for Dart before establishing his own special-purpose vehicle factory in Kansas City in 1952. From very small beginnings (8 trucks in 1953) Cline gradually became one of the most important makers of trucks for coal strip-mining. Two and three-axle trucks with similar styling to the example shown here have been made since the 1950s with Detroit and Cummins engines. This is a TD-1120 bottom dump coal-hauler for 40-ton loads. As well as rear and bottom dumpers Cline makes trucks with a hydraulic headboard that ejects the load without tipping. Cline prefers multi-axles and lots of 'small' tyres to lower the centre of gravity, increase braking capacity, increase traction, reduce overall size and lessen tyre replacement costs. The rear tandems are self-tracking and have rubber suspension.

LEFT
Chaseside agricultural tractor-based dumpers were once well known but outside the scope of this book. The firm also made wheeled loaders with Perkins and Ford V8 engines and were eventually acquired by J.C.B. In the mid-1950s they moved briefly into the heavier dumptruck field with the 5.5 cu yd struck capacity Rockmover. It had five speeds with reversible controls and a four-cylinder diesel.

LEFT
Cline introduced pivot-steering dumptrucks in the early 1960s and had made 169 by 1968. With four tyres on all three axles this T-60 could carry 60 tons. A two-axle version for 22-ton loads with Cummins 220 bhp diesel and Clark torque converter four-speed powershift transmission has been in production for 20 years and 35, 45 and 55-ton models are now also made. Between 1972 and 1979 Cline was owned by the ISCO Manufacturing Co whose name appeared on many of their trucks. But in 1979 T & J Industries bought ISCO and the Cline name has since been re-introduced.

ABOVE
Cook Brothers made trucks for the construction industry during the 1950s and the early
1960s, latterly as a division of the Challenge
concrete mixer firm under the name of
Challenge-Cook. They made a wide assortment of dump trailers and some special
Earthking tractors to pull them. Here we see
one in the late 1950s on the Navajo Dam
project. It carried 50 tons, which could be
unloaded on the move in nine seconds when
the bottom door in the Earthhauler trailer
was opened. The Earthking had Reo or
Cummins engines and six-wheel drive, and
production ended in the early 1960s.

CENTRE
Mass-produced chassis like this mid-1950s
two-stroke diesel Commer were seldom
suitable for arduous quarry life. However,
this was one of a pair with Pilot 7 cu yds
bodies that spent their life moving stone 850
yards from the quarry face at Moneymore,
Northern Ireland to the crusher. Each vehicle
handled about 300 tons per day and it would
be interesting to know how long they survived
the treatment. See Haulamatic for later
conversions of Commers.

RIGHT
A rather fuzzy photo from eastern North
Korea shows a mysterious giant 100-ton plus
capacity Consol dumptruck. Without details
of its technical specification it is difficult to
pinpoint the origins of its design, which
could be either Russian or Chinese via the
USA. It is interesting that largely unindus-
trialized nations should nowadays enter the
vehicle market with machines for making the
most of their natural resources. Tractors and
dumptrucks often come before trucks and
cars.

ABOVE

The County FC made in Fleet, England is in use both as a rigid dumptruck (with a nominal capacity of 16,000 lbs) and as an artic. The recent example shown here is unusual in being fitted with a hydraulic crane so that it can be self-loading. Power comes from a Ford 117 bhp diesel driving the four tractor wheels via a dual range four-speed gearbox giving 16 forward and 4 reverse ratios. The Thompson dumptrailer is of a type supplied for use with several makers of industrial tractor.

County FC tractors of the mid-1970s had a cab mounted at the centre point between the front wheels.

CENTRE

Around 1960 the famous Curtiss-Wright aircraft firm diversified into the rapidly expanding construction machinery business with a two-axle 300 bhp tractor suitable for towing bowl scrapers and dumptrailers. Soon afterwards they brought out a 375 bhp pivot-steer 35-ton capacity dumptruck. Unfortunately they found that the boom was short-lived and of benefit mostly to the established manufacturers with well proven products and extensive servicing networks.

LEFT

Founded in Romania in 1973, the DAC factory now produces giant 4 × 4 (twin tyres all round) half-cab dumptrucks, smaller full cab, forward control three-axle dumptrucks (some with simple angular cabs and some with MAN – licence cabs), the twin-engined T41.27 six-wheelers (270 bhp total), and the 170-100 D E shown here. This has a gvw of 170 tons, of which 120 tons is payload. It has a 905 bhp diesel and can travel at up to 50 km/h. Smaller engines in the ranges are MAN-based but the provenance of the larger ones is uncertain and may be the Polish Wola H used in some of the larger Belaz models.

MODEL 10S 10-ton capacity, 6.5 cubic yard body, 160 H.P. diesel engine, 5-speed transmission, 12.00 x 20 tires, hydraulic power steering, wheelbase 108", vehicle weight 20,000 lbs.

MODEL 15SL 15-ton capacity, 11 cubic yard body, 220 H.P. diesel engine, 5 or 10-speed transmission. Tires—12.00 x 25 front; 14.00 by 25 rear. Hydraulic power steering, wheelbase 156", vehicle weight 32,500 lbs.

MODEL 40T 40-ton capacity, 26 cubic yards, 450 H.P. diesel engine, torque converter and 3 or 4-speed transmission, tires 18.00 x 25, 24 ply, hydraulic power steering, wheelbase 206", vehicle weight 79,000 lbs.

MODEL 50T 50-ton payload, 31 cubic yard body, tandem rear axles, 600 H.P. diesel engine, torque converter and 4-speed transmission, 18.00 x 25 tires, hydraulic power steering, wheelbase 206", vehicle weight 88,000 lbs.

MODEL 802 24-ton capacity, 16 cubic yard body, 320 to 375 H.P. diesel engines, 10-speed transmission, torque converters optional. Front tires 14.00 x 25, 20 ply; rear, 18.00 x 25, 24 ply, hydraulic power steering, wheelbase 168", vehicle weight 46,000 lbs.

MODEL 25SL 25-ton capacity, 16 cubic yard body, 320 to 375 H.P. diesel engine, 10-speed transmission, torque converters and power shift transmission optional, 14.00 x 25, 20 ply tires front; 18.00 x 25, 24 ply rear. Hydraulic power steering, 176" wheelbase, vehicle weight 46,000 lbs.

MODEL 802B Tractor-trailer design. Capacity 48-tons, 32 cubic yard body, 320 to 375 H.P. diesel engine, torque converter and power shift transmission optional. Tires: front 14.00 x 25; rear 18.00 x 25, hydraulic steering, tractor wheelbase 168", vehicle weight 71,000 lbs.

MODEL 804B 64-ton capacity, 40 cubic yard end dump trailer body, 600 H.P. diesel engine, 10-speed transmission and power shift transmission, tires 18.00 x 33, hydraulic steering, tractor wheelbase 168", vehicle wt. 105,000 lbs.

MODEL 30S 30-ton capacity, 20 cubic yard body, 320 to 375 diesel engines, torque converters, 10-speed transmission or power shift transmission, hydraulic power steering, tires 18.00 x 25, 24 ply, wheelbase 132", vehicle weight 49,000 lbs.

MODEL 35SL Capacity 24 cubic yards, 450 H.P. engine, 3 or 4-speed transmission with torque converters, front tires 18.00 x 25, rear tires 18.00 x 33, hydraulic power steering, wheelbase 200", vehicle weight 61,000 lbs.

MODEL 50SBDT 50-ton payload, 61 cubic yard trailer, 320 to 375 H.P. diesel engine, 10-speed transmission or torque converters and power shift transmission. Tires: front, 14.00 x 25; rear tractor and trailer 18.00 x 25, hydraulic steering, tractor wheelbase 142", approx. weight 59,000 lbs.

MODEL 70SBDT 70-ton capacity, 90 cubic yard trailer body, 450 H.P. diesel engine, 10-speed transmission or torque converter and power shift transmission. Tires: front 18.00 x 25; rear tractor and trailer tires 18.00 x 33, hydraulic steering, wheelbase 156", approximate weight 83,000 lbs.

OPPOSITE ABOVE
By 1960 Dart offered an extensive range of 10 to 70-ton capacity models (see historical introduction for earlier types). Following its acquisition by the owners of Kenworth in 1958 it took on some of the former Kenworth models and made these, and its own, under the name KW-Dart.

OPPOSITE BELOW
The DJB had been a remarkable success story since the first was built in England's North-East in 1973. David John Brown had previously worked in forestry and for the Hunslet and Muir-Hill firms. Using Caterpillar components the DJB could be serviced around the world, and to date more than 90% have been exported (some 30% to North America). The 1000th DJB was sold in 1979 and capacity is now 500 per year. Two and three-axle versions are made, the one shown being a 1980 D550 for 55 short tons (50 tonnes) with 18-litre, eight-cylinder Caterpillar 336 kW (450 bhp gross) diesel and powershift four forward/four reverse transmission with torque converter. Drive goes to the front and middle axles, and suspension is hydraulic at the rear and oil/nitrogen on the front axle.

TOP
Here we see a mid-1960s 110-ton capacity Dart articulated truck with Cummins turbocharged V12 diesel developing 700 bhp. When it first appeared with 95 tons capacity in the early 1960s this was the largest truck in series production in the world.

CENTRE
Though still part of the PACCAR group, Dart resumed its old name in 1970 and went on to produce several colossal new models. A feature of them has been mechanical, rather than the diesel-electric drive of some of the 100-ton plus trucks of its rivals. With 4,000 dumptrucks to its credit up to 1980 Dart is one of the major producers.

Here we see a 1981 3120 model for 109-tonne (120 short ton) loads. It has rubber suspension, triple reduction axle, Detroit or Cummins engines of up to 1200 bhp and Allison six-speed transmission with torque converter.

BOTTOM
Like Cline, Dart now offers three axle dumptrucks to achieve a lower centre of gravity on smaller, cheaper tyres and more traction. Of 85 tons capacity and with 597 kW (800 bhp) Detroit or Cummins diesels, they are popular on the steep and slippery haul roads encountered when stripping coal. Of course tandem axle trucks are not new to Dart, who made them in the 1950s and 1960s. The recent 2085 model shown has Allison automatic transmission and Dart double-reduction tandem axles.

ABOVE LEFT
The 6 × 4 Automaster came in 15 and 22-ton capacity sizes. This is an Automaster 15 of 1962 with option of Cummins, Rolls-Royce or Leyland diesels of up to 178 bhp, whilst the 22 had Rolls-Royce or Cummins engines of 250 bhp output. Both types had SCG four-speed automatic (epicyclic) transmission, although manual gearboxes were available. The pronounced bonnet was the result of a set-back front axle to increase manoeuvrability. Production gave way to Douglas's speciality in aircraft and dockyard tugs.

ABOVE RIGHT
Variously known as Dutra and Mogürt (after the Hungarian vehicle exporting agency) the products of the Gödöllő Machine Engineering Works have included the G-116 10 T dumptruck since prototypes were developed in 1966. This was a 4 × 4 truck for 10-ton loads with a 5.2 m³ struck capacity and was based on a dumptruck produced for five years from 1961 by RABA. Both versions had Csepel six-cylinder 125 bhp engines. They had leaf springs front and rear and eight forward gears plus four reverse. Production is believed to have ended in 1973.

LEFT
Euclid set up its first factory outside America (in Scotland) in 1950 and was acquired by General Motors in 1953. Thereafter GM's Detroit two-stroke diesels were widely used, although other makes were available and indeed Rolls-Royce, Leyland and Cummins 170-220 bhp diesels were the only types offered in this Scottish-built F D Model. This is the classic shape of Euclid that varied little in appearance between the late 1930s and the late 1960s. It has a 10.6 cu yd struck capacity body, was for loads of 30,000 lbs and had a Fuller five forward speed gearbox, Euclid double-reduction rear axle and springs on just the front axle. Top speed was 25 mph. Shock loads during loading and running were cushioned by rubber buffers.

In 1968 GM were compelled to sell Euclid under monopoly law. White bought the American factories but GM carried on in Scotland under the name Terex (see Terex). White in turn sold Euclid to Daimler-Benz in 1977 and dumptrucks are now made in America, Belgium, Australia, South Africa and Canada. Shown here is a 1977 R-22 with Detroit or Cummins engines of 170 and 179 kW gross (228 and 240 bhp gross). Manual or automatic transmission was offered on this model, which was the smallest in the range until recently superseded by the R-25. Note the trailing arm, coil spring independent front suspension. Payload was 22 short tons.

Eimco, an American manufacturer of loading shovels, introduced at its British factory at Gateshead in 1960 an 850 model 9 cu yd pivot-steer dumptruck. It had drive to its front axle from a Leyland 0.600 150 bhp diesel and could climb a 1 in 4 hill with a 25,000 lb load. Top speed was 24 mph and at £5950 it was claimed to be £2000 cheaper than its nearest rival.

BELOW

In 1958 the respected British heavy truck maker ERF entered the dumptruck field with the 54G, the first production truck to feature disc brakes on its front wheels, although this feature soon gave way to drum brakes. It had a Gardner 5LW, 7-litre, 94 bhp diesel, although six-cylinder 112 or 150 bhp Gardners could be specified, when the model became the 64G. The body had a struck capacity of 5.35m³ (7 cu yds) and gross weight was 15 tons. A 1962 example is shown. Variations of the model continued through the 1960s and the 1970s latterly as the TJC 180 18 tons gvw truck with Cummins 240 bhp diesel and full width cab.

ABOVE LEFT AND RIGHT
Giant twin-engined Euclid trucks had included the 45-ton three-axle ILLD in 1951 with two 300 bhp Cummins diesels. In 1958 a three-axle tractor with two-axle dump trailer for Western Contracting Corporation with twin Detroit diesels totalling 850 bhp was the largest truck in the world, with a capacity of 150 tons. Here we see it and a twin-engined giant of 1961. The R-62 series 5LLD model 6 × 4 had six-cylinder Detroits totalling 672 bhp and Allison four forward two reverse speed torque converter transmission. Payload was 124,000 lbs, gross weight 232,000 lbs and struck capacity 40 cu yds.

CENTRE
The largest Euclid rear dump in 1983 is the R-170 whose colossal size can be appreciated by examining the nine-step ladders into the cab. The truck stands 5.69 metres (18ft 8in) high, 6.35 metres (20ft 10in) wide and 12.07 metres (39ft 7in) long. It has Cummins, Detroit or MTU (a firm partly owned by Daimler-Benz) 1194 kW gross (1600 bhp gross) diesels driving General Electric or Reliance alternators which power motors at each rear wheel. Struck capacity of the body is 71.1 m³ (93 cu yds). The R-170 suspension is by compressed fluid in cylinders at front and rear.

LEFT
Current Euclid CH-150 (150 short tons capacity coal hauler) has V12 783 kW (1050 bhp) gross output Detroit or V12 Cummins of similar output and six forward-speed Allison planetary transmission with automatic shifting. The bottom dumping trailer has a struck capacity of 137m³ (178.6 cu yds). The tractor portion is similar to the 100 short tons capacity R-100 dumptruck and like it has independent front wheel suspension. Having been owned by General Motors, White and Daimler-Benz, Euclid in 1984 was acquired by Clark (see Michigan).

ABOVE
As a specialized vehicle builder, Faun developed various trucks for the construction industry in Germany after the war and in 1950 offered an unusually large dumptruck for 20-tonne loads. By the late 1950s their largest truck was the K20/41 shown here. It had a V12, 16-litre, 250 bhp Deutz air-cooled diesel and six forward/one reverse constant mesh gearbox. The back axle was rigidly attached to the frame and had separated load-carrying and driving portions with planetary reduction in the hubs. Body capacity was 11m^3 (14.3 cu yds) and payload was 22 tonnes.

RIGHT
A K40/40 VW during construction about 1960. With a 40-tonne capacity it was the largest Faun dumptruck of its day. It had a 400 bhp Deutz V12, air cooled diesel and ZF six forward/two reverse ratio gearbox plus torque converter. Versions were also available with Deutz 340 bhp or Rolls-Royce 400 bhp diesels. Unusually for a truck of its size, the rear axle had leaf springs (two pairs, one above the other). Struck body capacity was 19m^3 (24.7 cu yds). The truck could climb a gradient of 36% (1 in 2.8) at 71 tonnes gvw.

ABOVE
An unusual machine in 1964 was this Faun L910/40V. It had a Deutz V10, 250 bhp diesel and was intended for 32 tonnes gvw (18.2 tonnes load). Three of the four axles were driven (the second steering axle was not) and a 6 × 6 version was also offered. Other unconventional dumptrucks at the time were special slag carriers with solid rubber tyres and underground side dumpers with two-way controls and steering on all four wheels. The latter had water-cooled Deutz 133 bhp diesels. Faun's most popular dumptruck in the 1960s was the forward control K10 (for ten-tonne loads) which had 4 × 4 and a six-cylinder Deutz air-cooled 125 bhp diesel.

LEFT
The Faun K80 first appeared in 1971 and could have Cummins 800 bhp or Maybach 1000 bhp diesels. Payload was 75 tons. Faun formed a link with Foden in 1974 which lasted for two years, during which the two firms marketed certain of each other's products. The K80 became the current K85.8, which has Cummins or Detroit engines of 596 kW (811 bhp) to 641 kW (872 bhp) with Allison six-speed powershift torque converter transmission. It has hydro-pneumatic suspension and a payload of 77 tons.

Recent Faun dumptrucks included two-axle models for loads of 24 to 85 short tons with engines of 169 to 596 kW. They also make the pivot-steering K 22.2 B shown here, which drives on both the outer axles (the rear one by hydrostatic motors) and can carry 22 short tons. It has a heaped capacity of 10.5m³. The Deutz air-cooled diesel develops 141 kW (176 bhp) and there is Allison powershift transmission. A version with 6 × 6 is also offered. Top speed is 50 km/h (31mph) and gradeability is 32%. Faun moved even more closely into the construction machinery field with the acquisition of the Trojan loader company in America in 1979 and the German Frisch firm a year later.

RIGHT
Fiat and its subsidiary OM does not make specific dumptrucks but there are numerous conversion specialists in Italy. As well as transmission and chassis alterations, they often fit their own rugged half-cabs and bodies. The example chosen is a late 1960s Minerva version of a 226 bhp Fiat 693/NA. It has Minerva's own ingenious Multico tipping gear which restricts the bulk of its stress to the hinged lifting frame. This allows a lighter sub-frame to be used and ensures that the ram is always at the right angle to avoid distortion.

TOP
Fully tracked dumptrucks are normally only used where minimal ground pressure has to be exerted, for example in the tundra or on marsh reclamation. There are various Canadian manufacturers of such machines, and here we see a Flextrack-Nodwell of about 1970. This firm is now associated with Foremost, which makes both tracked and wheeled off-road vehicles. The FN110 Diesel shown has Detroit or Perkins engines of up to 234 bhp (petrol engine optional) and five forward/one reverse gears. Gross vehicle weight is approximately 12 tonnes and payload 5 tonnes. Top speed is about 20 mph. Laden ground pressure is roughly 2 lbs per square inch.

CENTRE
Following the success of its earlier half-cab forward control trucks in January 1958 the Foden FRD6/45 was launched and the first prototype is shown here. It had a Rolls-Royce 12.17-litre, turbocharged, 300 bhp, six-cylinder diesel and manual transmission (although a three-speed gearbox and Twin-Disc torque converter were used on production versions and a Cummins diesel became optional). Payload was 28 short tons and gvw was 52 short tons. Body capacity was 18 cu yds and overall width 11 feet. The rear axle was semi-rigidly mounted, and the front one had a centre pivot and twin transverse leaf springs. Several of these giant trucks were built, but with competition from Scottish-built Euclids, English Aveling-Barfords and AECs, plus all the American rivals, production was not economically viable and it was discontinued in the 1960s.

BOTTOM
Four-axle dumptrucks have never been common because overall length usually has to be kept to a minimum for manoeuvrability and stability when tipping. For specific construction jobs these considerations sometimes do not apply and for harbour building in Dubai in 1968 several of these 40-ton gvw 8 × 4 Fodens were supplied. They had 27-ton payload rock bodies, Rolls-Royce Eagle 209 bhp six-cylinder diesels, nine-speed gearboxes and shields integral with the cabs rather than with the bodies. Several were still at work more than 10 years later, despite very arduous conditions.

In 1979 the two and three-axle Foden dumptrucks for 17–35-ton loads adopted this styling and such features as rubber suspension, torque converter automatic transmission in most models and Cummins six-cylinder engines of 250 to 420 bhp. Similar machines with more angular styling were also assembled at Foden's South African plant. In 1974 Foden's had extended their range by offering the larger Faun trucks, but this arrangement was shortlived because of currency fluctuations. In 1980 Fodens were acquired by PACCAR, who control Peterbilt, Kenworth, Wagner and Dart in the USA, and Foden dumptruck production was terminated, the last being sold in October that year.

CENTRE LEFT
Ford does not produce specific dumptrucks in any of its worldwide factories but several models have been converted by specialists over the years. One of the chief exponents in Britain was Vickers – AWD, who made 4 × 4, 6 × 4 and 6 × 6 versions in the 1950s and 1960s with heavy-duty frames and other components. Here we see an AWD 4 × 4 Ford Thames Trader with 5 cu yd body. Note the revised frontal treatment to keep the lights at legal height. Several civil engineering firms used these machines, and in the early 1960s McAlpine had several with low ground pressure Terratyres that could carry seven tons up to a gradient of 1 in 2.

CENTRE RIGHT
Floor have made special purpose FTF trucks in Holland since the mid-1960s, some of which have been used for earthmoving. Shown are a fleet of 1981 FD/FS 10.40D models with sand bodies each working at 50,000 kg gvw. 6 × 4 or 6 × 6 is available and the trucks have Detroit V6 turbocharged two-stroke diesels developing 238 kW (324 bhp) and Allison five-speed automatic transmissions. The model is also offered for hauling dump or other trailers and can have a V8 Detroit 304 kW (414 bhp) engine. Note the shields on the body and also attached to the cabs.

BOTTOM
The British Ford D Series came in for its share of conversion work to make it suitable for arduous construction site and quarry duties. This is one of 10 used in 1973 on a land reclamation scheme in Jersey. It has an oversize front axle and single tyre equipment all round to comply with the Island's width limit for vehicles. It was for 16-ton loads and had a Perkins 160 bhp, V8 diesel and Ford six-speed synchromesh gearbox. The reclamation project lasted over two years with the trucks working up to 14 hours per day.

DUMPTRUCKS
IN COLOUR

PRECEDING PAGE
At the start of 1983 Volvo acquired Kockum and the two names were combined. This is the complete range of rebadged Kockums at the time.

TOP
A rugged Foden working in 1970 for Bamburi Cement Company, Mombasa, Kenya. It had Cummins 220 bhp diesel and is still in use.

BOTTOM
A 1981 Wabco Haulpak 408-008 with O+K loader. An idea of its size can be gauged from the built-in ladder required to reach the modular cab. The Haulpak range first appeared in 1957 and pioneered the vee-shaped body for reduced loading height and extra stability.

TOP CENTRE SPREAD
A pair of final-pattern Fodens introduced in 1979 with Cummins engines
and Allison transmissions in a typi-
cally tough working environment.

CENTRE LEFT
Atkinson half-cab dumptrucks with
Gardner or Cummins engines enjoyed
some sales success in the 1960s.

TOP LEFT
A colossal O+K hydraulic shovel
fills a Terex in the days when this
dumptruck firm belonged to General
Motors.

BOTTOM LEFT
A pair of KW-Dart rear dump haulers
shown at work in 1967 with extra-
large rock bodies and cab protectors
on the tractors rather than trailers.

BOTTOM CENTRE SPREAD
Unit Rig's Lectra Hauls did much to popularise diesel-electric drive from their inception in 1963. This is a late 1970s 1600 bhp Mark 36 for 170 short ton loads in its 85m³ (112 cu yards) heaped capacity body.

CENTRE RIGHT
Clark's Michigan division made Cummins powered pivot-steer dumpers in the 1950s and 1960s. In 1984 Clark acquired Euclid.

TOP RIGHT
A gigantic Michigan wheeled loading shovel at work in Iran in the 1970s with a Faun truck.

BOTTOM RIGHT
An Italian Astra BM 2 SA of the late 1970s for 10.9 tonne loads with a reversible driving position and 4 × 4. It has a Detroit 175 bhp diesel and ten speeds both forwards and backwards.

TOP
One of the earliest BM-Volvo 4 × 4 pivot-
steer dumptrucks developed in 1966 being
used with a loader from the same manufacturer. The maker's name was changed to
Volvo BM in 1973.

BOTTOM
A recent view of 1050 bhp Cummins or
Detroit engined Dart 3100 for 100 short tons
being loaded by a Dart 600 C 24´ short ton
capacity pivot-steer shovel with 725 bhp
Cummins diesel.

TOP
Caterpillar-powered DJB six-wheelers working on an American canal construction project with a Caterpillar ladder. The D 550 introduced in 1978 for 50 tonne loads is the largest pivot-steer machine produced in the world.

BOTTOM
A 1979 International 635 bhp Pay Hauler 50 ton capacity 350B model. This machine is still in production with the Payhauler Corp. and is unusual for its 4 × 4 with twin tyres all round.

TOP
The Rimpull is so named because of its mechanical drive with triple or quadruple gear reduction in the rear axle which applies maximum torque at the wheel rim. This recent example is for loads of 120 short tons.

BOTTOM LEFT
An elderly Kockums (with the s now discontinued) employed on the Ayvacik dam project in Turkey. The first Kockums was made in 1961 and the 420 first appeared in 1965. It is still in production as the 425.

BOTTOM RIGHT
A current Dart 4160 bottom dump hauler for 160 ton loads. It has a 1050 diesel with Allison six forward speed t mission.

ABOVE LEFT
Like many other mass-produced trucks, Commers have been modified for arduous work. One of the most ingenious conversions is shown here. Realizing the pounding that the transmission of a site vehicle takes, Haulamatic of Ilkeston, UK in 1961 fitted a Commer with Allison automatic transmission. With a scow-ended rock body it was found to be able to do most of the work expected of heavy-duty, and much more expensive, dumptrucks. It was originally conceived as an on/off road vehicle, but because most customers used their automatic transmission Commers largely on-site, the machine was re-designed in 1968 for more arduous duty.

ABOVE RIGHT
The revised Haulamatic of 1968 shown here had a purpose-built chassis, no frills half-cab. and planetary double reduction ten ton capacity rear axle. It had a Perkins 6.354, 5.8 litre, 120 bhp diesel and Allison six forward speed automatic transmission. Gross weight of the GP8 was 16 tons and top speed was 47 mph. The transmission had already been tried in previous Haulamatics in 10,000 hours of use and gave greatly reduced downtime as a result of no clutch repairs, greater reliability than manual gears and smoother operation that helped prop shaft, differential and half-shaft life.

LEFT
In 1969 the GP8 was re-designated as the 4–10 and joined by a three-axle model, the 6–15. As the numbers imply, this was for a load of 15 tons and was later joined by a 20-ton sister. The 6–15 had a Perkins V8 derated from 180 to 165 bhp for longevity, and a six forward ratio Allison automatic transmission. It had leaf spring suspension, the rear ones supporting rocking beams for maximum bogie articulation. Both rear planetary reduction axles were driven and had an air-operated differential lock for maximum traction on wet sites.

In 1979 Haulamatic developed a pivot-steered truck to supplement their rigid six chassis and the prototype is shown here. It had a payload of 22 tons, a heaped capacity of 14 m³ (18 cu yds) and a gvw of 37.5 tons. Production versions known as the A625, have drive to the front and middle axles via a ZF torque converter and six forward/three reverse transmission. The engine used is the Detroit 6-71N, developing 157 kW (210 bhp). Haulamatic also make a 4 × 4 pivot-steered A420 and became part of the Clarke Chapman engineering group.

In 1983 the NEI Thompson division of Northern Engineering Industries acquired control of the firm and output of about 100 trucks a year continued to be sold through Blackwood Hodge's John Deere division.

CENTRE
Hayes of British Columbia made very heavy duty trucks for the typical operating conditions in the West Coast and Northern Canadian logging, quarrying and construction industries. This is their 1968 HD-400 truck available with various Caterpillar and Detroit engine options in the 250-450 bhp range and Spicer, Fuller or Allison gearboxes. The chassis was of all-bolted construction.

Mack acquired a two-thirds interest in Hayes Trucks Ltd in 1969, but after five years Hayes passed into PACCAR's hands and ceased production in 1975.

BOTTOM
The Heathfield division of Centrax Ltd, makers of axles, gearboxes and gas turbine motor blades in Devon, UK, introduced a Perkins-powered 7 cu yd dumper in 1966. It is shown here in 1970 form, when it was known as the DF-20 and complied with Construction and Use Regulations which permitted use on the road.

A key feature was maintenance-free rubber suspension. The Perkins 6.354 developed 120 bhp and there was a David Brown five-speed gearbox with overdrive giving up to 41 mph. The rear axle was a Centrax hub-reduction unit and payload was 20,000 lbs.

ABOVE AND LEFT

Heathfield quickly moved out of the medium-sized dumper field and in 1973 had 19 and 28 short ton models with Leyland and Cummins engines followed by other engine options. This is a DE50 model in the lunar landscape of the Cornish china clay industry. It had a 280 bhp (gross) Cummins diesel and led to the H19 and H28 and current H20, H30 and H33.

In 1978 Heathfield considered re-entering the on/off road market with a rigid six-wheel dumptruck but did not go beyond the prototype stage, and in the following year made pivot-steer 6 × 6 dumpers based on the discontinued Swedish Nordverk. The prototype 20-tonne capacity H2200 is shown here. It had a Cummins VT555C 219 bhp diesel, Allison five forward/one reverse torque converter transmission, with rubber suspension on the Kirkstall front and Eaton rear axles.

It was to be sold by SLD in place of the Haulamatics they had previously handled, but there was insufficient demand for both types.

LEFT

The German heavy truck maker, Henschel, was briefly associated with Saviem-Renault in 1961/3, and this is an HS34 from that period. It had a gvw of 34 tons (20-ton payload), 10m³ body, 6 × 6, a 204 bhp Henschel six-cylinder diesel and two-range gearbox giving 12 forward and 2 reverse ratios. The Rheinstahl group that owned the Hanomag truck firm took over Henschel in 1964 and, after merging the two, sold a majority interest to Mercedes-Benz in 1969. In the early 1970s the separate identity of Hanomag-Henschel disappeared.

TOP
The Japanese firm Hino began to make ZG half-cab dumptrucks in 1953, and here is a mid-1950s example. It has a six-cylinder, 10,857cc, 175 bhp diesel, and six-speed constant mesh gearbox. Payload was 13,500 kg (29,700 lbs) and struck body capacity 6.8m³ (8.9 cu yds). Two unusual features were the choice of six alternative factory paint schemes and the fact that a hook on the cab shield allowed the engine to be lifted out for a major overhaul (the hydraulics then being powered separately). Both axles had semi-elliptic springs and the rear one had hub reduction gearing. The ZG with only slightly revised appearance was still in production in 1982, then with an 11,581 cc, 210 bhp diesel.

CENTRE
A 1964 Hino ZM220 6 × 4 with 10.2-litre, six-cylinder, 190 bhp diesel, spring parking brake, exhaust brake and leaf springs all round. Transmission consisted of a five-speed main box and four-speed auxiliary box, both with constant mesh. These together gave 20 forward ratios from crawler to 59 mph. 4 × 2 and 4 × 4 versions with similar cabs were also made and 130 of the former were sold to the Peruvian Government in 1964. In 1966 Hino merged with Toyota and continues to be the group's heavy truck specialist.

BELOW
International Harvester's construction equipment division made bottom dump and wheeled scraper hauling units in the 1950s, and two-axle rigids from late in the decade. The trucks were known as Payhaulers and were the 65 with 250 bhp for 19 tons and the 95 with 335 bhp for 24 tons. Here we see a 495 Paywagon of around 1960 with 375 bhp diesel and 27 cu yd struck capacity bottom-dump trailer. The Payhauler rigids looked similar, apart from having smaller twin tyres at the rear and full-width cabs.

ABOVE
The Chinese Jiefang CA390 was introduced recently by the No 1 Motor Vehicle Factory, Changchun City, who also make a 100-tonner whose name can be translated as 'beautiful peak'. The CA390 is for loads of 60 tonnes and has a Chingfa V12, 29.56-litre, 537 kW (720 bhp) diesel. Top speed is 50 km/h and gvw is 105 tonnes. The vehicle is probably based on Russian designs.

LEFT
In 1964 International introduced their ingenious PH180 which had 4 × 4, equal weight distribution front and rear, ultra short 3.56 metre (11ft 8in) wheelbase and twin tyres all around. The eight 'small' (18.00 × 25) tyres cost less than six normal dump-truck tyres and helped to reduce the centre of gravity and spotting height. Payload was 45 short tons and top speed 34 mph. In 1970, and perhaps at other times, the trucks were assembled for IHC by Hendrickson of Chicago. Shown here is one of a fleet of five with locally produced Robert Hudson bodies working for the Swaziland Iron Ore Development Co in 1971. They had V16 Detroit 560 bhp diesels and Twin-Disc powershift torque converter transmissions. For a more recent version of the same concept see the 350B in the Colour Section.

In 1982 International's dumptruck division became a separately owned company under the name Payhauler Corporation. International's construction machinery division was bought by the Dresser Corp for a reputed 100 million dollars.

ABOVE

There have been several ingenious attempts to make self-loading dumptrucks. Elsewhere we show the Wakefield truck, and there have also been several smaller types, particularly for working in confined spaces underground. Joy Manufacturing Co in America are well-known for mining equipment, but in 1967 they made this large Transloader TL 110 to be equally at home in quarries. It had a Cummins diesel and could carry 34,000 lbs in its 12.5 cu yd body at up to 20 mph. It had pivot-steering and a sideways operating position.

RIGHT

Kaelble made their first dumptruck in about 1950, and here we see a little changed 6 × 6 model of 10 years later. Their largest trucks of the time, for 24 tonnes on two axles and 32 tonnes on three axles, could have Kaelble's own V8 diesel. This was first offered in 1951, developing 200 bhp, but by 1961 output was up to 300 bhp. However, as shown in this sales leaflet, the smaller models had straight-six engines.

KAELBLE

3-Axle Raer Dumper
KDV 22E8 and KDV 22E6T

240 and 270 HP   **Payload up to 22 300 kg**   **Capacity up to 15 cbm**

Engine

Manufacturer Carl Kaelble GmbH.,

	Type GO 130 a	alternatively	Type M 130 sT (with turbo-charger)
combustion method	prechamber		prechamber
output	240 HP at 1600 rpm	output	270 HP at 2100 rpm
	resp. 255 Gr. HP (SAE)		resp. 287 Gr. HP (SAE)
max. torque	107 mkg at 1200 rpm	max. torque	97 mkg at 1400 rpm
No. of cylinders	8, V-shape	No. of cylinders	6, in line
cylinder bore/stroke	130/180 mm	cylinder bore/stroke	130/180 mm
displacement	19,1 ltr.	displacement	11,945 ltr.
working method	4 stroke cycle	working method	4 stroke cycle
lubrication	forced feed lubrication	lubrication	forced feed lubrication
lubrication oil filter	disc type filter	lubrication oil filter	micro filter

🔆 6199 a   🔆 6200 a

lube oil pressure		3,5 atü
cooling		waterpump and fan
cooler		gilled radiator
total cooling water capacity		76 ltr.
oil cooler		tubular cooler, Längerer & Reich
fuel supply		Bosch fuel injection pump
		with feed pump
injection pressure		approx. 125 atü
fuel consumption		185 gr./HPh
air filter		oil bath type

Transmission

shifting gear	mech. stage gear
manufacturer	ZF Friedrichshafen
type	AK 5—140
distributor gear	2-stage toothed gear
type	ZA 801 or ZA 800
number of speeds	10 forward, 2 reverse
ratios:	
shifting gear	3,35/2,2/1,42/1,0/0,585, 4,85
distributor gear	1,825/0,829
arrangement of shift lever; near driver's seat	

Clutch

type	multiple disc dry
	friction clutch
manufacturer	Fichtel & Sachs
model	LA 2/70 HA 6 or G 2/70 KR
diameter	380/200 mm
transmittable torque	140 mkg
total clutch area	3270 cm²
release power in clutch	190 kg
method of operation; hydraulically	

Axles

number of axles	3
driven axles	3
front axle: axle housing of electric	
steel casting with front axle drive;	
wheel hub with planetary gear	
rear axles	
Banjo axle with rear axle gear	
ratios:	
front	1 : 2,16 × 1 : 3,714
rear	1 : 12,9 or 1 : 15,35

brake cylinder, front	on axle arm
number	2
size	A 100 DIN 74282
piston diameter	100 mm
piston power	290 kg
stroke	140 mm
hand brake	mech. brake acting
	on rear axles
operation	by hand lever
reinforcement	2 spring chambers
type of spring chamber	
	SV-DZB 150-180 A 10
spring power	2 times max. 500 kg
stroke	max. 180 mm
diameter of brake drum	
front	440 mm
rear	480 mm
width of lining	
front	100 mm
rear	160 mm
brake area	
front	1215 cm²
rear	4385 cm²
third brake	exhaust-engine-brake
operation	pneumatic, foot actuated

Steering

type	mech. with hydraulic booster
	steering
model	ZF-spindle-hydro-steering
ratio:	25,7:1
hydr. torque of steering shaft	715 mkg
pump pressure	100 kg/cm²
oil pump	ZF-pump
conveying capacity	17 ltr./min.

Brakes

foot brake : air brake acting on all wheels	
brake pressure	5 atü
air bottle capacity	240 ltr.
capacity of add. air bottle	20 ltr.
brake cylinder rear	on axle housing
number	4
size	A 125 DIN 74282
piston diameter	125 mm
piston power	460 kg
stroke	140 mm

🔆 6196

ABOVE
Kaelble dumptrucks were re-styled in the mid 1960s and here we see a 4 × 4 KV50S of 1966 hauling a side-dump trailer. It had a turbocharged Kaelble V8 diesel developing 425 bhp and could haul at least 80 tonnes (the tractor unit normally being a 50-tonne dumptruck chassis). Twelve of the 34 and 50-tonne models were built in the course of 21 months, showing the very specialist demand for such large trucks and explaining why Kaelble abandoned their own engine production soon afterwards and bought proprietary engines (mostly from Mercedes-Benz) from then on.

CENTRE
This is how the smallest rigid two-axle Kaelble model looked in 1972. The K20B had a 20-tonne payload, 13m³ heaped capacity and a 177 kW (265 bhp gross) Mercedes-Benz diesel. Most of the range had all-wheel-drive but the K20B had 4 × 2 with optional retarder brake and exhaust-heated body. Kaelble made quite an extensive range of other construction equipment at the time, including crawlers, tractors, rollers and loaders and in the mid-1970s took over the rival Gmeinder range.

LEFT
In Kaelble's current range are both rigid and pivot-steer trucks. The latter include 15 to 45-tonne capacity models, and here we see a 1976 example of the smallest of them, the SK16. It has a low profile for use underground and has a Deutz V8 129 kW (176 bhp) diesel driving Hägglunds hydrostatic wheel motors in all four hubs. Top speed is 8.4 km/h, struck body capacity is 5m³, gradient ability is 30% and overall height is a mere 2.25m. The largest model has a choice of V12 Mercedes-Benz engines of up to 20.9 litres capacity and 386 kW (580 bhp) output. Intermediate models use Mercedes and MAN engines and all now go under the name Kaelble-Gmeinder.

The first Kockum dumptruck from Sweden, the LT-2A, was made in 1961, and at the last count was still at work in Yugoslavia after 48,000 working hours carrying 3 million tons of rock. The LT-2A shown here was slightly revised in 1965 as the KL-420, using a Scania six-cylinder 225 bhp turbocharged diesel and dual-range five forward speed synchromesh gearbox with planetary reduction rear axle. Struck capacity was 9.5 m³ (12.5 cu yds) and payload was 20 tonnes (22 short tons).

The KL-420 was made from 1965 to 1973, and its larger 440 sister from 1967 to 1972, although the outwardly similar 442B for 32 tonnes is still in production.

TOP
The Kamaz hails from a factory in the geographical centre of Russia on the banks of the Kama River, where potential production is said to be 150,000 trucks per year. Introduced in 1978 with technical and production assistance from US Ford, Renault and others, the first trucks were heavy-duty 6×4 models. The on/off road 5511 dumptruck has a gvw of 22,360 kg, a tilt cab and a V8, 126 kW (220 bhp), 10.85-litre diesel with two-range, four forward/one reverse ratio gearbox. Body capacity is 7m³.

CENTRE
Kenworth heavy-duty trucks have frequently been used as the basis of dumptrucks since the 1930s, and in the mid-1950s specific half-cab models were made, including the two-axle 400 bhp 803 model for 32-ton loads. This is its slightly smaller 802 sister with its usual 300 bhp diesel removed and power provided instead by General Electric wheel motors fed from overhead wires. It was one of a fleet bringing ore out of a mine where exhaust fumes could have been hazardous.

BOTTOM
Since 1945 Kenworth has belonged to Pacific Car and Foundry, who bought Dart in 1958 and concentrated dumptrucks under the KW-Dart name until 1970, when the two firms resumed their separate identities. Although Dart are now the dumptruck specialists in the American group, Kenworth still make some giant dump models as this 1981 33 foot-long, 548 model, 6 × 4 coal truck shows. It had a 450 bhp Cummins six-cylinder turbo-diesel, Allison automatic transmission and Rockwell axles giving 120,000 lbs capacity on the tandem and 28,000 lbs at the front.

Named after the mining town of Kiruna in Sweden, where they were produced, Mining Transportation Co made various pivot-steer shuttle dumpers in the 1960s. These were mostly for underground use, although larger models were added by 1973 when the K-250 shown here was made. It had a 240 bhp, 9.6-litre, turbocharged Volvo diesel, torque converter transmission, drive by hub reduction to the front wheels and a body capacity of 28m³ for loads of 40 tonnes. Other models included the 35-tonne 162 bhp K-162 and the 65-tonne K-500.

LEFT
Kockums make various 4 × 4 and 6 × 6 pivot-steer models, and this is a 412 T working in 1977. It had 4 × 4 with Scania 7.8-litre, 127 kW (173 bhp) diesel and Clark powershift torque converter transmission with four ratios both forward and backwards. There is hub reduction gearing in each wheel, and the frame pivots vertically and horizontally to keep all wheels firmly on the ground. Struck body capacity is 8.3 m³ (10.8 cu yds) and payload 16 tonnes (18 tons). The T version (for tunnels) has exhaust purifier and optional rubber-lined body to minimize noise.

Kockum 540 was new in 1981 and built of specially light high tensile steel to make it the lightest 36-tonne (40 short ton) capacity truck available. Unladen weight is 25.8 tonnes and struck body capacity is 17.2m³. The six-cylinder Cummins turbocharged diesel develops 335 kW (456 bhp gross), and there is a six forward/one reverse ratio Allison powershift gearbox with torque converter. There is hydropneumatic suspension and hub reduction rear axle. Top speed is 65 km/h and width, height and length are respectively 3.73m, 3.72m and 8.08m.

BELOW
An example of Komatsu's first model from Japan in 1951 is shown in the historical introduction. This is the uprated HD180 which replaced it in 1968 and is still in production in outwardly similar form. It is shown being loaded by a large IHC Hough Payloader in about 1975, when its specification included manual five forward/one reverse gears, 230 bhp gross diesel, 18 tonnes (20 short tons) payload, 10.7m³ (14 cu yds) struck capacity and leaf spring suspension.

Since 1961 most Komatsus have been powered by Cummins engines built under licence by Komatsu in Japan.

Koehring are old established American construction equipment-makers whose cranes have been produced in Britain for many years by Newton Chambers under the initials NCK. Dumpers were made from the 1920s and from 1931 a large half-track Dumptor model was offered. Although dumpers are outside the scope of this book, by the mid-1960s several of Koehring's Dumptors had grown to 15 tons capacity, and they were followed in the late 1960s by the true dumptruck shown here. Details of its technical specification are not available.

CENTRE
The largest current Komatsu is the HD1200 which is available in M form with automatic planetary gear and torque converter, eight forward/one reverse transmission, or alternatively with electric motors in the rear wheel hubs. In both cases a Cummins V12 895 kW (1200 gross bhp) diesel is used and payload is 120 tonnes (132 short tons). Suspension is by hydropneumatic cylinders on all wheels and there are oil-cooled disc brakes at both front and rear. Struck body capacity is 46m³ (60 cu yds). Height to the top of cab is 5.17m, width is 6.55m and length is 10.885m.

BELOW
The Russian KrAZ 256B has been sold in Britain since 1971 as a BelAZ. This model started in the 1950s as the Yaaz with two-stroke six-cylinder diesel. When re-designed as the 256B it acquired a V8 four-stroke, 14.866-litre, 265 bhp diesel with part synchromesh five-speed, two-range gearbox. Top speed was 65 km/h (42 mph), load was 15.24 tonnes (33,600 lbs) and the struck capacity was 8m³. For highway use it could legally be used with a reduced payload but the majority worked continually on site. The model is still in production.

61

The German steel, armaments and heavy vehicle firm of Krupp made its first dump-truck in 1951 (see introduction) and this is their MK17 of around 1960 which had replaced the very similar 15-ton capacity, 185 bhp Cyklop model. The MK17 had Krupp's own five-cylinder, 7.27-litre, two-stroke, 200 bhp (220 bhp gross) diesel and ZF constant mesh six forward speed gearbox. Payload was 17 tonnes (37,500 lbs) and struck capacity 9m³ (11.7 cu yds). It had 4 × 2 with hub reduction gearing in the rear wheels. Maximum speed was 40 km/h (25 mph) and gradient ability 37.2%. Suspension was by leaf springs on both axles.

CENTRE

The largest Krupp of 1959 was the AMK22C7 for 39-tonne (85,998 lbs) loads. Here we see one converted in 1961 to tow a side-dump trailer for autobahn construction work. It had 4 × 4 and a Krupp two-stroke, uniflow scavenged, 10.17-litre, 310 bhp diesel. There was a six forward speed ZF gearbox and two speed transfer box. Top speed was 32.6 mph and gradient ability 31.5%. The dump body had a capacity of 26m³ and payload was nominally rated at 40 tonnes. As with the MK17, there was an engine brake in addition to air brakes on the wheels. Suspension was by leaf springs on the front axle and rubber on the rear, hub reduction axle.

RIGHT

From 1963 Krupp gradually replaced its two-stroke engines with Cummins four-strokes that they built under licence in their own factories. Although two-strokes were still found in the MK18, 23 and 27, in 1966 the MK30 shown here had a 15.57-litre V8, 430 bhp, 'C' (Cummins) motor from 1963 as an option to the 280 bhp seven-cylinder Krupp unit. The latter was mated to a ZF six-speed manual gearbox, while the former had a six-ratio Allison transmission. The truck had 4 × 2 with hub reduction and rubber suspension at the rear with conventional semi-elliptics on the front axle.

ABOVE
Krupp also made heavy-duty on/off highway trucks until 1968, when it was reorganized under a complex war reparations scheme. After that it gave up all types of dumptrucks and trucks except for truck-mounted cranes. The three K360 trucks being exported from Germany had 6 × 4 although 6 × 6 AK versions were offered and there were also 4 × 2 and 4 × 4 trucks using this cab. The engine was a Krupp-Cummins V6, 9.65-litre diesel of 230 bhp, and payload was 15.3 tonnes. The stripes painted on many Krupp site vehicles made them more clearly visible.

LEFT
The Unit Rig and Equipment Co of Tulsa, Oklahoma and Niagara Falls, Ontario has made giant dumptrucks since 1963 under the name Lectra Haul. Here we have one of their earliest machines, with a body capacity of 36 cu yds and a payload of 55 tons. A 600 bhp diesel drove a generator and electric wheel motors. While diesel-electrics are Lectra Haul specialities, a 100-tonner was built in 1965 with International Harvester Solar 1100 bhp gas turbine-electric drive. After two years and 6000 hours work it was still in successful use. The machine shown had pivot-steering, but most subsequent Lectra Hauls have been two-axle rigids.

LEFT
Some 3,000 Lectra Hauls have been made, including rear dumps, articulated bottom dumps and the unusual BD-30 ore-hauler introduced in 1979. This has four equally spaced tyres at front and rear, the outer front ones pivoting round suspension columns to give a 26-metre turning circle. Length is 10.67 metres, height 5.71 metres and width 6.35 metres. Reasons for the unusual shape are to increase stability, improve weight distribution, remove the jack-knife risk of articulated haulers and give a better ratio of unladen to laden weight. A 1200 bhp diesel-electric generator powers wheel motors and is mounted above the rear wheels.

ABOVE

The M-200 Lectra Haul shown here is the largest two-axle dumptruck currently in production in the world, the first of which was sold in 1968. In 12-cylinder 2475 bhp EMD (a division of General Motors)-engined form, it is 14.63 metres (48ft) long, 7.8 metres (25ft 6ins) wide and 6.45 metres (21ft 2ins) high. The struck capacity of the body is 84m³ (110 cu yds) and total weight of the laden vehicle is 325 tonnes (716,600 lbs), and payload is 181.4 tonnes (200 short tons). There are two electric rear wheel motors, the fuel tank holds 3028 litres (800 gallons) and suspension is by rubber-cushioned Dynafloat columns.

RIGHT

Various heavy-duty Leyland models, notably the normal control Super Hippo and Super Beaver, have been used as dumptrucks, but most specific chassis have been left to group member Scammell, and more recently, Aveling-Barford. The Super Hippo also came with forward control and Ergomatic tilt cab, and here we see one of a fleet of 20 being loaded by novel means on a construction project in North Borneo in 1967. They had 10 cu yd Telehoist bodies with six-speed gearboxes plus crawler ratio.

TOP
This 1966 Comet has a 4 × 4 conversion by Scammell, although earlier examples had been converted by AWD. It could have 115 or 131 bhp Leyland diesels and five or six-speed gearboxes with two-range transfer boxes. Both front and rear axles had hub reduction. Payload plus body was 5343 kg (11,782 lbs) in rough off-road conditions. Comet dumptrucks were also made in India and kept the Leyland 1940s cab style.

ABOVE LEFT
This current Indian-produced Ashok Leyland is a 6 × 4 Hippo for 15.5-tonne loads. It has an 11,093 cc, six-cylinder, 180 bhp Ashok Leyland diesel and nine forward/two reverse gears. It has hub reduction axles, a struck body capacity of 9m³, and central trunnion-mounted rear leaf springs with conventional semi-elliptics on the front axle. Ashok Leylands use components produced wholly in India.

ABOVE RIGHT
The replacement for the normal control Super Hippo export truck in 1980 was the Leyland Landtrain, available with 4 × 2 or 6 × 4, Leyland or Cummins diesels of 212 or 290 bhp and six or nine-speed gearboxes with hub reduction axles. Shown is a 30-29 dumptruck for 30 tonnes gvw or 65 tonnes gtw if working with a trailer. A 20% overload factor is built into the model, which is in widespread use in Africa.

LEFT
The MAN semi-forward control chassis has been widely used in the quarrying and construction industries since the mid-1960s and is still in production in modernized form. Shown is a 1965 1580 DHK available with 6×4 or 6×6 for 16-ton loads. A 20-ton capacity 2180 DHK with 233 bhp diesel was also offered. Over the years heavier versions, first with 256 and then 320 bhp diesels, have been built, and the 30.320 DHAK can gross 30 tonnes off the road (17.7 tonnes payload) or 38 tonnes with semi-trailer, and has a 16-litre V10 diesel.

An even larger dumptruck is sold under the MAN name in several markets and is described under ÖAF, MAN's Austrian subsidiary.

CENTRE AND BOTTOM
The Russian MAZ factory has made dumptrucks on many of its heavy duty chassis since it opened in 1947, including in recent years the 4-cu yd, 7-tonne, 503 model with 180 bhp V6 and tilt cab. It has also made some giant machines starting in the early 1950s with two and three-axle rigid dumptrucks, and two-axle tractors towing rear dump semi-trailers. All were similar to the 530 (made 1957-63) and 4×2 525 (made 1951-67) examples shown, and were quoted as having engines of 375/450 bhp. Whether all used the same engine with different rates of fuel pump and governor setting is uncertain, but the most commonly quoted specification included 38.8-litre V20 diesel and a top speed of 20 mph.

RIGHT ABOVE
Mack was one of the most important dumptruck pioneers and examples of its early vehicles can be seen in the introduction. Its early postwar range started with the LR and LV models with Mack's new hub reduction Planidrive axles. Two and three-axle rigids and hauling units were made with power-steering, air-operated clutches and 200-275 bhp Mack diesels. The chassis were made from I-section alloy-steel girders. Here we see an LR 33-ton capacity side-dump tractor unit which in rigid form was sold as a 15-ton capacity dumptruck with Mack or Cummins engines of 170-205 bhp.

RIGHT
The Belgian off-road and specialist truck manufacturer MOL has a relatively short history, having sold its first vehicles in 1966. Many of these looked similar to the 6×6 Magirus-Deutz of the time and, like them, used Deutz engines. Deutz diesels still figure prominently in the MOL range and here we have a 6×6 dumptruck available with V6 or V8 diesel of 170 or 230 bhp, and five or thirteen-speed gearboxes. This 26-tonne (58,300 lbs) gvw example dates from 1977, and has a gangway round the engine bay to simplify maintenance.

ABOVE
The Mack LRVSW from 1952 could carry 34 short tons and weighed the same amount unladen. It was powered by a 1486 cu in V12, Cummins 400 bhp diesel. There was a Mack constant mesh four forward/one reverse ratio gearbox with two-speed range-change (or Westinghouse torque converter) and Plani-drive tandem. Suspension was by leaf springs and rubber shock insulators. Struck capacity of the Heil rock body was 24 cu yds, and height to the top of the canopy when tipped was 25ft 2ins. Overall length of the monster was 31ft $3\frac{1}{8}$ins, and width 11ft $2\frac{1}{8}$ins.

RIGHT
The M series of Mack dumptrucks began in 1960 and the previous L series was gradually replaced by it in the early 1960s. The 15 and 18-ton versions used Mack diesels, but above that weight Cummins or Detroit diesels were specified. This is a 1963 M-65X with choice of V12 engines in the region of 600 bhp. It had double leaf springs at front and rear to give progressive suspension when unladen and laden. There were six forward ratios with torque converter and Planidrive rear axle. Body capacity was up to 42 cu yds and payload was 65 short tons. For a time in the 1960s Muir-Hill marketed some of the M series in Britain.

An unusual concept in 1973 was the Mack-Pack which had pivot-steering, 4 × 4, disc brakes, a rear-mounted Detroit V12, 475 bhp diesel (450 bhp Cummins optional) and eight-speed Clark powershift transmission with torque converter. It could carry 40 short tons and its bottom-dump body had a struck capacity of 19.1m³ (25 cu yds). There was rubber suspension on the front axle and the driver's cab was comfortable and independently rubber-mounted. Top speed was almost 60 km/h (40 mph) and gradient ability 35%.

BELOW LEFT
The offset cab had become a feature of Mack heavy-duty trucks by the late 1930s and here is an example of its latest application on a current DM model. It gives extra visibility in difficult site conditions. The DM range covers 149–336 kW (200 to 450 bhp) models with Mack, Cummins and Caterpillar engines. There can be one, two or three axles at the rear and gvw goes up to 46,700 kg (103,000 lbs). Transmissions are Fuller 9 to 15-ratio Roadranger types.

BELOW RIGHT
The familiar current range of normal control, all-wheel drive Magirus vehicles with Deutz air-cooled engines stems from 1956, when such models as the 6 × 6 Saturn 150AK dumptruck first appeared. Nowadays they have 188 or 235 kW (256 or 320 bhp) V8 or V10 diesels and are suitable for loads of up to 17,180 kg. For a time they were marketed in Britain by Seddon in the late 1960s and then assembled here briefly. In 1975 Magirus joined the Iveco Group and was responsible for Fiat, Unic and OM normal control site vehicles, some with water-cooled engines from the other members of the group. This 1979 photograph shows some of a large fleet supplied to Russia being used in very difficult conditions to build a railway in Siberia.

ABOVE AND RIGHT
Mitsubishi's Fuso heavy truck division in Japan made a half-cab forward-control dumptruck very similar to the Hino ZG in the early 1960s, and also a 6 × 6 W11D normal control truck of typical US Army appearance. Both used Mitsubishi six-cylinder 8.55-litre diesel rated at 145 and 160 bhp for loads of 7 and 10 tonnes respectively. The 4 × 2 truck was classified T52 and had five forward and three reverse gears, while the 6 × 6 had a two-range, four-speed gearbox. The T52 had a top speed of 48 km/h (29 mph) and gradient ability of 43%. The 6 × 6 could have various rear and side dump bodies, had a top speed of 56 km/h (35 mph) and gradient ability of 35%.

CENTRE
The Marion crane and excavator firm in America entered the giant truck market in 1971 with its V-Con model range for loads of 250 tons and upwards. The four-abreast wheel arrangement is also used by Lectra Haul, but in the case of the V-Con the electric wheel motors receive their current from diesel generators underneath the centre part of the body. Alco (American Locomotive) and EMD (GM's railway engine subsidiary) diesels of up to 3000 bhp are used. The 1975 270-ton capacity 3006 model shown is 28ft wide and therefore has to be delivered to most sites in sections for final assembly there.

RIGHT
Various heavy-duty Mercedes-Benz chassis in the 1950s, particularly 4 × 4 models, were used as the basis for dumptrucks. The trend has continued since the 1960s with the three-axle LK/LAK models. As in the case of MAN, the semi-forward control layout has been maintained for rugged, no frills vehicles long after the on-highway versions have been replaced. Here a mid-1960s LAK 2620 demonstrates its hill-climbing ability (45.3%) thanks to a crawler speed of 2.9 km/h at optimum engine revs. It had a 230 bhp gross, 10.81-litre, six-cylinder diesel, ZF six-speed gearbox with transfer box, 6 × 6 and a load capacity of 18.9 tonnes (41,650 lbs). The rear springs were centre-trunnion mounted.

LEFT
Mitsubishi's current dumptruck chassis is the NV113K with 6 × 4 and V8, 14,886 cc, 206 kW (280 bhp) diesel and six-speed partially synchromesh gearbox. Its weight with body is 9,685 kg (21,350 lbs) and its gvw is 25,400 kg (56,000 lbs). A forward control (cabover) FV version is also made. The Fuso name has gradually disappeared since the two vehicle-making parts of Mitsubishi were re-united in 1964 following postwar reparation, when attempts were made to reduce the size of the giant armaments and engineering firm.

CENTRE
The American construction machinery firm of Michigan, whose wheeled loaders were made for a time in Britain by AWD, have also made Cummins powered two-wheel haul units for scrapers and pivot-steer dumpers. Transmissions are by Clark, who are the parent company of Michigan. After six years' development they entered the two-axle rigid dumptruck market in 1968 with the T-65 for 65-ton loads. It had a Cummins 700 bhp gross diesel as one of its many engine options and a prototype was tried by Costain on a British opencast mine from 1967. Suspension was by Clark Air-Hydro columns similar to those found on aircraft landing gear. One suspects that Michigan did not pursue the project with total commitment because of objections from the Clark's other customers for dumptruck components.

BELOW
Muir-Hill made Britain's first tractor-based dumpers in 1927 and a wide assortment of dumpers and wheeled loaders over the next 50 years. True dumptrucks have seldom been produced, although there was a 5m³ (6½ cu yd) 20B after World War II with AEC 7.7-litre, 96 bhp diesel, road equipment and cab, followed by a similar 18B with Ford 96 bhp engine. In addition to rigid dumpers Muir-Hill adopted the Camill pivot-steer machine, shown here, in 1966. It had Ford or International power units of 96 and 70 bhp respectively and could carry up to 9072 kg (20,000 lbs) in its 5.5m³ (7 cu yd) body. Later heavy dumpers have been limited to a few imported Macks and to heavy-duty trailers towed by Muir-Hill industrial tractors. The 1968 20 TD had 4 × 4, 127 bhp and hauled a four-wheel 20-ton capacity trailer that could be unhitched in 30 seconds.

J&P HARWOOD
PLANT HIRE
SAHAM TONEY
NORFOLK
J&P HARWOOD
PLANT HIRE

The Norwegian Moxy was developed in the mid 1970s and 38 were built in 1974/5 before series production started in 1976. In the next six years more than 600 were sold, and here we see a 1978 D16 at work in England. It had a six-cylinder, turbocharged 7.79-litre, 165 kW (221 bhp) Scania diesel and four speed forward and reverse Clark powershift gearbox with torque converter and 6×6. Struck body capacity was $9.6m^3$ and payload nominally 22 tonnes. The machine and its newer stable-mates, the D16B Super and 6200S, have pivot-steering and rear wheels attached to gearcases on 'walking beams' that are free to swing round a central drive axle housing for equalized ground contact.

RIGHT
A current Russian MoAZ all-wheel drive dumptruck for 20-tonne loads. It has a V8, 14.86-litre, 220 kW (300 bhp) YaMZ turbocharged diesel. MoAZ vehicles are made by the Mogilyev construction machinery plant, which has made dumptrucks for approximately 20 years. This 6507 model has been in production since 1979 and has a six forward ratio semi-automatic gearbox plus torque converter. Both axles have double reduction gearing.

CENTRE AND BELOW LEFT
The Japanese Nissan firm has built dumptrucks on its heaviest truck chassis in the past but now has two models built solely for the purpose. They are the WD23 half-cab, two-axle, 23-tonne capacity models with V10 350 bhp diesel, and the WD18 for 18-tonne loads. The WD18 is unusual in retaining a standard truck cab despite its large size (7.73m long and 2.99m wide). It has a 10.3m³ (13.1 cu yds) struck body capacity and V8, 300 bhp diesel with six-speed constant mesh gearbox and double reduction axle with planetary hubs. It has semi-elliptic front and rear suspension and an unusual tubular front axle (the WD23 differs in having independent trailing arm front suspension and Allison automatic transmission).

BELOW RIGHT
The Swedish Nordström has been made since 1975 and features Dunlop Pneuride air suspension on the front axle with rubber suspension on the rear bogie, six-wheel disc brakes, rear axle lift for unladen running, 50 km/h top speed, pivot-steering and drive to the front and middle axles. Load capacity is 25 tons and the exhaust-heated body holds 10.3m³ (struck). Power comes from a 10.4-litre Caterpillar 210 bhp diesel driving through an Allison five-speed automatic gearbox. This view shows the chassis ability to pivot in two planes simultaneously.

ABOVE

The Swedish Nord-Verk differs from many pivot-steer dumptrucks in having forward control with half-cab. It has been made since 1968, and when the 140B, shown here, was made in 1976 it featured a Volvo 6.73-litre, six-cylinder 175 bhp diesel with Clark power-shift transmission. The body's struck capacity was 10.4m³ and could carry 22 tons. The rear wheels were carried on centrally mounted gear cases and all six wheels were driven. Disc brakes were introduced in 1976 and the front axle was centrally pivoted so that the chassis steering point only had to move laterally. At a gross weight of 38 tons, a 23% loose-surfaced hill could be climbed.

CENTRE

One of the pioneer pivot-steered 'small' dumptrucks came from Northfield of Osset in Yorkshire. Starting with an F7 model (shown) in 1961 they developed the larger F9 (9 cu yds) two years later. Both machines had front-wheel drive and choice of Ford or Perkins diesels of up to 120 bhp with manual gearbox and torque converter. In 1965 came the F12 with Perkins 120 bhp diesel and 20-tons capacity, and in 1968 a larger prototype with 185 bhp V8 Cummins diesel and Twin-Disc transmission was built. Northfield, like Whitlock, were unlucky in being ahead of most of their rivals and therefore had to convince operators that pivot-steer dumptrucks had a future. It was an uphill struggle against traditional dumptrucks in those days, not won until many more brands had proved themselves in off-road work.

LEFT

An ÖAF Tornado of the mid-1960s for export to the Eastern Bloc. It had a heavy-duty coal body for strip mining and was powered by a Cummins NH 250, although a Leyland 0.680 was more typical, or one of ÖAF's own engines in lighter versions.

MAN's Austrian subsidiary ÖAF builds specialist vehicles for sale under both its own name and that of MAN. Their Jumbo model (1978 example shown) has MAN tilt-cab and V10, 16-litre, 320 bhp diesel with ZF 16-speed or Fuller 13-speed transmission and 6×6. Gross vehicle weight is 38 tonnes or up to 150 tonnes with trailer. As befits its name, the Jumbo is large with a length of 8m, a width of 2.49m and a cab height of 3.135m.

BELOW
The well known Oshkosh truck firm from the town of that name in Wisconsin which was itself named after a 19th century Indian chief, has made all-wheel-drive trucks since 1918. Many have been used for road construction and quarrying over the years. This tractor with bottom-dump semi-trailer dates from the early 1950s and was the smallest of a series of haul units that by the end of the decade included a 60-ton half-cab model with Cummins 525 bhp diesel and 37-cu yd trailer. All these tractors had the unusual feature for their day of 4 × 4 with torque proportioning differentials.

The Oshkosh W-2800 of 1958 had Cummins 320 or 335 bhp diesels, or a Hall-Scott 368 bhp motor running on butane. The similar W-2803 had Cummins 380 bhp turbocharged diesel, and all used Allison four forward, two reverse ratio transmissions with torque converters. Payload was 30 short tons in bodies ranging from 17 cu yds for iron ore to 28 cu yds for bauxite. Gross weight was 60 short tons and suspension was by semi-elliptic springs with helpers at front and rear. These trucks were the largest with all-wheel-drive before the arrival of the eight-tyred Caterpillar, and featured Oshkosh double-reduction axles with torque-proportioning differentials.

For the construction industry Oshkosh made on/off highway transit mixer chassis and these, utility trucks and export models soon ousted dumptrucks from their range.

CENTRE
The Pacific Truck and Trailer Company of North Vancouver has specialized in trucks for the logging industry since it was founded soon after World War II. In recent years it has branched into trucks for heavy haulage and the oil exploration and construction industries. Since 1970 it has belonged to International Harvester who in 1983 sold it to a subsidiary of Britain's Inchcape Group.

The P-12-W shown has a V12 Detroit 475 bhp diesel with Allison six-speed powershift transmission. The body holds 50–55 cu yds of coal and can carry 40 tons.

BOTTOM
The Spanish Pegaso factory has made half-cab dumptrucks alongside its regular commercial vehicle range for several years. Shown is a recent 3078 model for 36 tonnes gvw off-highway operation.

It has a turbocharged 10.5-litre Pegaso 191 kW (260 bhp) diesel with ceramic-lined clutch and ZF nine-speed gearbox.

Top speed is 58–64 km/h, depending on axle ratio, and maximum gradient ability is 42%. The truck has semi-elliptic front suspension and sprung, trunnion-mounted 'walking beams' at the rear.

RIGHT
The Italian firm of Perlini started making
dumptrucks in 1962, and this is a T20 of that
time with 20-ton load capacity and 253 bhp
Detroit diesel. It was followed by a smaller
15-ton model with Fiat 210 bhp six-cylinder
diesel and six forward speed gearbox. A 32-
ton model came in 1967, and a 40-tonner
with 440 bhp Detroit engine, in 1968. The
latter year saw Scania engines fitted in some
models for the first time, and in 1970 the
thousandth Perlini dumptruck was sold.

BELOW
Perlini's largest current dumptruck is the
DP955, which has Detroit or Cummins
diesels of 746 kW (1000 bhp) and Allison six
forward/one reverse ratio transmission with
torque converter. It has oleo-pneumatic
suspension cylinders at front and rear, double-
reduction rear axle with planetary hubs, and
a load capacity of 90.7 tonnes. Gross weight
is 154 tonnes, struck body capacity is 40 m^3,
and overall dimensions are length 10.51m,
width 5.15m and height to the top of cab
4.86m. The DP955 has disc brakes and
engine retarder, and a top speed of 63.7km/h.

It took 10 years for Perlini to sell their first
1500 dumptrucks, but in the following 10
years they built 5000 more and are now one
of the most important producers.

LEFT
Peterbilt, like Kenworth, Dart and Foden, is a member of the Paccar group and makes heavy duty chassis which are widely used in the construction and opencast mining industries. It built its first dumptruck — a chain-drive, three-axle model — during World War II, and here is a 1977 successor with bulk-coal body. Behind it is an ISCO (a name briefly used for Cline trucks). Peterbilts have the usual wide choice of proprietary components and engines offered by the American custom-truck builders, this example having a 55,000 lbs capacity tandem, 13-speed gearbox and Cummins 350 bhp diesel.

CENTRE
The Czech 6 × 6 Praga V3S has been in production since 1952 with few changes, except that it is now made in the Avia light truck factory. This 1980 example has a Tatra air-cooled 7.41-litre, 73 kW (98 bhp) six-cylinder diesel and two-range, four-speed gearbox. Payload is only 5.3 tonnes, or less in rugged terrain, but this is a nominal rating based on its military vehicle origins.

BELOW LEFT
South Africa's only indigenous heavy-truck maker was Ralph. Many other firms assemble a similar assortment of proprietary components but they started as subsidiaries or agents of overseas firms such as Foden, Leyland, ERF and Oshkosh. Ralph Lewis made his first Ralph in 1967/8 and production ended four years later with less than 50 sold. A small batch of these 50-ton capacity ore haulers was made with Cummins V12, 700 bhp diesels and eight-speed transmissions with torque converters.

BELOW RIGHT
Renault are recent recruits to the pivot-steer concept and this machine is produced for them in Inchy en Artois by SA E Panien et Fils. The tractor is powered by an MWM six-cylinder, 6234cc, 99 kW (140 bhp) diesel with synchromesh 12 forward/reverse speed gearbox. The two foremost axles are driven and capacity is 24 tonnes.

For earlier examples of Renault dump-trucks see SAVIEM.

ABOVE
As a supplier of replacement parts to users of
giant dumptrucks, Rimpull was in a good
position to know what could go wrong. For
more than 20 years it perfected an axle
incorporating quadruple or triple reduction
to reduce torque stress in the transmission
and instead concentrate the highest of them
where they were actually wanted, at the
wheel rim. Hence the name Rimpull adopted
for the complete dumptrucks they launched
in 1975. The CW-150 bottom-dump coal
hauler has Detroit or Cummins 1000 or 1050
bhp diesels, Allison six-speed powershift
transmission, and suspension by either steel
semi-elliptics or Firestone 'Marsh Mellow'
rubber springs. Capacity is 150 short tons
and the struck body holds 175 cu yds.

CENTRE
Like Dart, Rimpull favours mechanical rather
than electric drive on trucks of 100-tons
capacity and upwards. This is their RD-100
of 1982. It has a similar mechanical specification to the CW-150, including quadruple
reduction drive axle. Note the radiator
position behind the cab for maximum
protection and seclusion from clogging dust.

Although by no means the largest Rimpull,
the RD 100 for 100 short-ton loads neverthe-
less dwarfs the Chevrolet service truck. The
RD 100 can have Detroit or Cummins V12
1050 bhp diesels and Allison six-speed
gearbox with torque converter. The circles
above the lights in each case are the ends of
Donaldson engine air cleaners.

Other Rimpull models in 1982 included
bottom-dump coal haulers up to 200 short-
tons capacity, three-axle rigid dumptrucks to
100 short-tons capacity, and two-axle trucks
from 75 short tons up to 130 short tons.

RIGHT
The Swiss firm of Saurer made the S4C
heavy-duty tipper chassis with few changes
between 1938 and 1960. A similar machine,
but with 4 × 4, continued at their Austrian
factory with eight-cylinder, 10.6-litre, 160
bhp diesel for 8-tonne loads during the
1960s. During the 1970s both two and three-
axle Saurer chassis were used for dumptrucks
with Saurer six-cylinder engines of up to 330
bhp.

LEFT

From Jan 1st 1983, Saurer and the small FBW specialist truck-building firm were controlled by Daimler-Benz, and Saurer and FBW chassis were gradually phased out in favour of Mercedes-Benz assembly for the Swiss market. This D330 Saurer dates from the time of these changes and is a special 6×4 dumptruck built for the Swiss Army. It has a 243 kW (330 bhp) Saurer diesel and is for 25 tonnes gvw (plus another 20 tonnes on a trailer).

CENTRE LEFT

SAVIEM came into being in 1955 with the merger of several French commercial vehicle-makers, including SOMUA, Latil and Renault. SOMUA had developed two and three-axle dumptrucks, and these carried on into the 1960s as SAVIEMs with SOMUA-Lanova, 150 bhp (180 bhp when turbocharged) six-cylinder diesels and 10 forward/two reverse SOMUA ratio gearboxes with double reduction axles.

The 18.25-tonne gvw M T P model of 1964 shown here had a 6m³ struck capacity, while the three-axle 25.25 tonne M T P V held 9m³. A trailer dump version of the latter could gross in excess of 35 tonnes.

Renault took over Berliet in 1974 and from 1979 both the SAVIEM and Berliet names disappeared, to be replaced by that of Renault.

CENTRE RIGHT

The British firm of Scammell (see historical introduction) had made heavy-duty tippers before World War II and in 1949 introduced the 4×4 Mountaineer. The component parts of a Scammell Sherpa chassis are shown here, including the spiral bevel, and epicyclic back axle also used on the Mountaineer. However, unlike the latter, the Sherpa had 4×2 and forward control (its cab was the same as the Himalayan shown). The Sherpa appeared in 1959 and had a 161 bhp six-cylinder 11.1-litre diesel by Leyland, who had acquired Scammell in 1955. Capacity was 8/9 cu yds (20 tons gvw), later increased to 9/11 cu yds (22½ tons gvw).

LEFT

The 6×4 Scammell Himalayan was new in 1961 and was for loads of 18 tons (12/14 cu yds) within a gvw of 30½ tons. The 11.1-litre six-cylinder Leyland diesel developed 200 or 185 bhp, and there was a Leyland six forward/two reverse plus crawler ratio gearbox. There were leaf springs at the front and rubber-bushed walking beams at the rear.

A full-width cab version was also offered. The Himalayan was replaced by the 690 Dumptruk (see AEC and Aveling-Barford), which was produced at Scammell in the late 1970s as the LD55 Mk II.

ABOVE
The Scammell Contractor, introduced in 1964, has been widely used for all types of heavy haulage. As a rigid 6 × 4 dumptruck it has been used at 57 tons gvw by Hebden Mining in Australia with Cummins 380 bhp diesel and 50 cu yd coal body. The side-dump artic shown here in England in the early 1970s worked at 85 tons gross and had a Rolls-Royce Eagle 305 bhp diesel, eight-speed semi-automatic gearbox and double reduction rear axles. Some early Contractors used AEC diesels, as found in the largest Dumptruk and hauled ore trains from Australian mines at up to 160 tons gross. The Contractor was modified as the S24 in 1980 and is now available with 6 × 4 or 6 × 6 and Cummins 350 bhp diesels.

CENTRE
Scania-Vabis had produced some producer-gas-driven dumptrucks in World War II (see historical introduction). Subsequent dump-trucks were on short wheelbase versions of its normal heavy duty chassis, like this 1966 DL76 with 195 bhp Dll engine and ten-tonne payload.

A new normal control (conventional) cab was adopted in 1972 and both two and three-axle chassis using it were available as dumptrucks with engines such as the DS14 334 bhp turbocharged unit and range-change, ten-speed gearbox. From 1968 the trucks were known simply as Scanias, and engines ran up to 388 bhp in the 1980s and were also used by Kockums.

RIGHT
Introduced in 1969 as the Shanghai SH 32 and subsequently re-designed as the SH 380 in the light of operational experience, this is another Chinese dumptruck. It has a Shanghai V12, 25.7-litre, 298 kW (400 bhp) diesel and three forward/one reverse gears. Load capacity is 32 tonnes and gvw is 54 tonnes. Top speed is 46 km/h and series production is believed to have commenced in the early 1980s.

LEFT

Developed in Rhodesia and tested in African mines in the late 1950s, the Shawnee-Poole system consisted of a conventional farm/industrial tractor towing a dumptrailer via an ingenious swan-neck arrangement. Produced in South Wales, the concept was one of the first key steps to the universal acceptance of articulated machines. Many other firms made similar machines using proprietary tractors and they are rather outside the scope of this book. But the 20-ton capacity Shawnee-Poole shown here had its own purpose-built tow-unit. The first, in 1968, used County 4 × 4 tractors with optional Sisu hydrostatic trailer-wheel motors, but then came this SF338 4 × 2 tractor with Perkins V8, 163 bhp diesel and automatic torque converter transmission with planetary drive axle. The body held 10.33m³ (13½ cu yds).

CENTRE

Sisu in Finland had made trucks since 1931 and heavy-duty ones since the mid-1950s. Its only venture into purpose-built dumptrucks took place around 1960, although subsequent machines have been built on three-axle normal control trucks. The 1960 K-36 shown here had six-cylinder 11.1-litre Leyland 160 bhp or Rolls-Royce 8.1-litre four-cylinder diesel, developing 183 bhp or 200 bhp when turbocharged. It had a two-range, five-speed gearbox and double reduction rear axle. Payload was 18 tons and struck capacity was 8m³. Top speed with the lowest axle ratio was 77 km/h, and maximum gradient ability was 46.5%. There were semi-elliptic springs at front and rear and air brakes on both axles.

Sisu also makes hydrostatic wheel motors and these have been used on several pivot-steer machines from other manufacturers.

LEFT

The Czech firm of Tatra made unusual heavy vehicles before World War II with backbone chassis and independent suspension that helped to give them good off-road capabilities. In 1942 came a similar range but with air-cooled diesels. The V12 version shown here continued in production for 20 years, and this is a 1957 example. It is a Type 111 DC-5 with 14.82-litre, V12 diesel developing 180 bhp. Payload was 10-12 tonnes, and gvw 20 tonnes. The struck body capacity was 5.19 m³ (6¾ cu yds). A similar machine, the T148, is still made today with 6 × 6, modernized cab with wrap-round screen, swing axles and V8 12,667 cc, 212 bhp air-cooled diesel. Body capacity is now increased to 9m³ and payload to 15.3 tonnes at 26 tonnes gross. A variant with British Motor Panels cab is sold in West Germany by Semex.

ABOVE LEFT
The Stavostroj T-180 from Czechoslovakia in 1966 had a Tatra 928 air-cooled diesel of unspecified output. Capacity was 12 tonnes in both side and rear dump versions, and bodies held 353 cu ft. A scraper version with additional rear power pack was also made.

ABOVE RIGHT
The Canadian firm of Sicard in French-speaking Quebec Province, made various off-highway trucks before being acquired by PACCAR in the mid-1960s, who soon discontinued Sicard production. In the late 1950s, when owned by the French Schneider steel and armaments firm, dumptrucks looking rather like Autocars were built including the T-6456 shown here.

From 1960 Sicard assembled KW-Dart dumptrucks in Canada, using their own chassis and cabs, but output was only about 20 per year.

The Tatra 813 series joined the normal control range in 1967 and is still produced in 4 × 4, 6 × 6 and 8 × 8 forms. Its V12 air-cooled diesel has grown in capacity and output and in the 1977 form shown here delivered 201 kW (270 bhp) from 18.48 litres. The cab tilted for engine access. There was a ten forward/two reverse speed gearbox plus two-speed transfer box doubling the ratios.

Payload was 25.6 tonnes and gvw 36 tonnes. The eight-wheel, swing-axle suspension had conventional leaf springs with centrally pivoted singles on each side taking care of the rear bogie. The 813 was, and indeed still is, one of the most unusual designs of off-road truck or heavy haulage tractor.

Terberg started by reconditioning ex-World War II military trucks left behind in Holland. During the 1960s it gradually became a manufacturer in its own right. Current production is 350 chassis per year and there are 140 employees. A high proportion of Volvo components is used including, in most cases, a Volvo cab. However, the F 1900 shown here has Terberg's own half-cab. It is an 8 × 8 machine with Volvo 233 bhp, six-cylinder TD 100A diesel and eight forward/one reverse Volvo synchromesh gearbox plus two-speed transfer box and Faun hub reduction axles.

The vehicle can operate off the road at 38 tonnes gross and with the 16.5m³ body shown can carry 22 tonnes.

It has rubber-suspended walking beams at the rear and semi-elliptics at the front supplemented by air bellows.

CENTRE
When General Motors sold its Euclid division to White in 1968 it was compelled to discontinue dumptruck production in America until 1973. But production continued in Scotland and at other GM plants under the new name of Terex. This is an early 1970s R-35S with 368 bhp Detroit V12 diesel and Allison six-speed, semi-automatic gearbox. Struck capacity was 17.8 m³ (23⅓ cu yds) and payload was 31752 kg (70,000 lbs). Top speed was 65 km/h (40 mph) and suspension was by leaf springs all round. A similar machine is still produced by Terex in Scotland (where the workforce amounts to some 2000 people) and by Hindustan Motors in India.

BELOW
The year 1974 saw the arrival of one of the biggest rigid dumptrucks — the 350-ton capacity Terex Titan. It had a 3,300 bhp diesel, of a type normally found in rail locos, and electric drive. The tyres were 11½ feet high and the ten used weighed 69,000 lbs and contained enough rubber to make nearly 6,000 average car tyres. The body when tipped was as high as a six-storey building. In 1977 there was talk of a 550-ton capacity model, although this was probably the old Titan uprated.

Famous for its giant heavy-duty military and oilfield trucks the British firm of Thornycroft supplied several of its chassis for use as dumptrucks. In the 1950s these were mostly Trusty 6 × 4 normal control models or Big Bens with either forward or normal control. The Big Ben shown here in Africa about 1958 had Thornycroft's own 11.33-litre six-cylinder 155 bhp diesel and eight-speed constant mesh gearbox. Payload was 21 tonnes (46,250 lbs) and gvw 31.75 tonnes (70,000 lbs).

In 1952 Thornycroft had offered a 4 × 2 dump trailer hauling version of their 250 bhp Antar with giant earthmover tyres but this probably never entered production.

CENTRE
The normal control Big Ben was available in the 1950s and 1960s initially with Thornycroft's 11.33-litre diesel in 200 or 230 bhp form but after the AEC takeover in 1961 usually with Cummins or Rolls-Royce diesels. Transmission was three-range, four-speed constant-mesh manual or, in the 1960s, eight-speed semi-automatic or Allison three-speed with torque converter. The 15-cu yd dumptruck version for 33.6 tonnes (74,000 lbs) gvw was supplied in considerable numbers for export (Goa had a big fleet) and was used in Britain by the National Coal Board.

Following the Leyland takeover of AEC, Thornycroft concentrated on gearbox production plus a few specialist vehicles until its factory was sold in 1969. Thereafter some Thornycroft vehicles were assembled by Scammell.

BELOW
A new design from Thornycroft in 1960 was a 4 × 2 or 4 × 4 20 tons gvw dumptruck looking very much like Scammell's Sherpa. Here we see a 4 × 4 being put through its paces. It had a Thornycroft 170 bhp diesel and was mechanically similar to the Nubian chassis, which had been used in large numbers in and after World War II. Payload was rated at up to 13 tons and sales were very small and not pursued after the AEC takeover in 1961.

RIGHT
Unic is the French member of the Fiat dominated IVECO group and nowadays its normal control tippers are Magirus-based but with water-cooled engines. However the former bonneted range, dating from the 1950s continued for a time after the Fiat takeover in 1966. This 6 × 6 Unic-Fiat Izoard 27–66 had hub reduction axles, an eight speed gearbox and Saurer injection system, 10.8 litre, 270 bhp, V8 diesel. Gross weight was 22.7 tonnes.

An enlarged Unic V8 continued in some models until 1975, latterly with outputs of up to 350 bhp, but by then cabs and many other components were common to Fiat or Magirus.

The British firm of Unipower made a speciality of converting two-axle trucks to three axles. In 1937 it added 4 × 4 forestry trucks using Rzeppa constant velocity drive joints, for which it held the British rights. By the late 1960s the demand for both conversions and normal control (conventional) forestry trucks was dwindling and a forward-control load-carrying Invader was developed. Here we see a 1971 example with Perkins 170 bhp V8 diesel being used in articulated form at 28 tons gvw. Very few were built, although larger 4 × 4s for use as airfield crash tenders became a Unipower speciality.

In 1980 General Motors sold Terex to the German IBH construction machinery group, in which the British firms Powell Duffryn and Babcock International held an interest of over 20%. The current dumptruck range includes 17–120-ton two-axle rigids and 150-ton articulated coal haulers. Detroit or Cummins engines are used, with Scanias in some of the smaller models. Shown is the 33-11D with V16 Detroit, 24.1-litre, 626 kW (840 bhp) diesel and Allison six-speed manually controlled electric shift gearbox with integral torque converter. It has nitrogen/oil suspension cylinders (independent at front) with drum brakes at front and oil-cooled disc brakes at rear. Payload is 77.1 tonnes (170,000 lbs) and gvw is 131.8 tonnes (290,800 lbs).

ABOVE AND CENTRE

The Bolinder Munktell engineering firm that Volvo acquired in 1950 made a BM-Volvo tractor with dump trailer in 1963, and in 1966 developed from it the pivot-steer machines shown here. These DR 631 models had 4 × 4 with unequal-sized wheels. Ten thousand BM-Volvo dumptrucks (mostly six-wheelers) were sold by 1981 and did much to popularize the pivot-steer concept (although they certainly did not pioneer it, as claimed by Volvo).

The name BM-Volvo became Volvo BM in 1973. Volvo truck chassis have, of course, also been used as the basis of on/off road dumptrucks over the years, notably the three-axle F86 and the N10 (1974 290 bhp 17.5-tonne capacity example shown).

BELOW LEFT

New in 1981 was the Volvo BM 5350 with 157 kW (213 bhp) six-cylinder 6.73-litre diesel and five forward-speed planetary gearbox with automatic change and torque converter. Drive goes to the front and middle axles, both of which have disc brakes (drums on the trailing axle). The 5350 has rubber suspension and the standard body holds 9.4m³ (12⅓ cu yds) struck. Payload is 20 tonnes (44,000 lbs) and gvw is 35.5 tonnes (78250 lbs). Top speed is 48 km/h (30 mph) and as an optional extra a rear axle lift is available for unladen running.

A smaller 861 model developed from the original six-wheel 860 (of which 1000 had been sold by 1972) is made for 31.9 tonnes (70325 lbs) gvw with 5.48-litre 125 kW (170 bhp) six-cylinder diesel.

RIGHT

This remarkable Trolly-Dump of the 1950s was developed jointly by LeTourneau and the Anaconda Co. A LeTourneau speciality was electric wheels and this 75-ton capacity dumper had four, each developing 400 bhp.

They were fed from an overhead cable most of the time, but when at the loading face were run from a generator powered by a 335 bhp diesel. This generator also provided alternating current for braking, steering and for the 130 bhp tipping mechanism.

ABOVE
1956 LeTourneau-Westinghouse Tournapull model Bs. At that time the firm made the D for 11-ton loads, the C for 22 tons and the B for 35 tons. The latter had Detroit or Cummins engines of 335-360 bhp and Allison powershift or Fuller manual gearboxes. Struck capacity was 23 cu yds, and the body was dumped by an electric motor and cables. Turning width was 35 feet and there were air-operated disc brakes on all wheels, assisted by an electrical retarder.

The RG LeTourneau Co had been one of the great American earthmoving machinery pioneers (an earlier pivot-steer dumper is shown in the historical introduction). It had made an electrically controlled, petrol-driven scraper in 1923 and the first rubber-tyred tractor-drawn scraper in 1932.

ABOVE

The LeTourneau-Westinghouse Haulpaks were remarkably advanced when introduced in 1957. The offset cab with its forward-slanting windscreen was widely copied, as was the body shape, which allowed a lower centre of gravity. Other features included oleo-pneumatic suspension and a limited-slip differential that put up to three times the power to the rear wheel that had the best traction. By 1962, when this photograph was taken the range included 22, 27 and 32-ton capacity models with 290, 335 and 375 bhp diesels respectively. In 1965/6 the largest Haulpak could carry 105 tons and had a British-built Dorman V12,930 bhp diesel. In 1967 the world's largest dumptruck was claimed to be a diesel-electric Haulpak.

RIGHT

In 1972 the LeTourneau name was discontinued in favour of Wabco (a contraction of Westinghouse Air Brake Corp). As well as being produced in North America, there were plants in other countries including Australia, and Belgium. More recently Wabcos have also been made under licence in China. This Haulpak 65 was made in Belgium and is shown by the Brussels Atomium. It had Hydrair suspension and a Cummins V12, 635 bhp diesel. Top speed was 71 km/h (48 mph) and gvw was 99 tons. Other models in the early 1970s included 35, 50 and 85-ton payload mechanical drive Haulpaks and 120 and 150-ton capacity trucks with diesel-electric drive and engines of up to 1325 bhp (Detroit V16 of 39.1 litres capacity). A feature of the diesel-electric models from 1965 was that the complete power packs could be hoisted out in one unit on a sub-frame for rapid servicing.

LEFT

The largest Haulpak of all was tested from late in 1971 and entered production in 1974. In the next 10 years roughly 50 of these 3200 models were sold. The specification at the outset included GM EMD V12, 127.6-litre, 2000 bhp, two-stroke diesel driving a generator and two electric motors. The rear wheels had planetary hub reduction. Payload was 181 tonnes (200 short tons) and the struck body capacity was $75m^3$ (99 cu yds). Principal dimensions were length of 15.39m (50ft 6ins), width 6.88m (22ft 7ins) and height 5.31m (17ft 5ins). Total loaded weight was 330 tonnes (727,550 lbs). The capacity was later uprated to 235 tons and power to 2475 bhp.

CENTRE

As well as an extensive range of rigid and trailer-dump Haulpaks, Wabco currently produces the 170 Coalpak with 80% interchangeability of parts with the Haulpak 170C. It has greater stability than the typical articulated coal hauler and better gradient ability (40% unladen) because of two-thirds weight on the drive axle. It also has a lower and wider body for easier 'spotting'. Technical features include rear-mounted 1194 kW (1600 bhp), V16 Detroit or Cummins diesels with electric drive. There is Hydrair suspension, bottom-dumping, a top speed of 71 km/h (44 mph) and a struck capacity of $149m^3$ (195 cu yds) with a payload of 170 short tons. It is 17.23m (56½ft) long, 6.93m (22¾ft) wide and 5.49m (18ft) high.

BOTTOM

The Wagner Mining Equipment Co of Portland, Oregon, USA was founded in 1958 to make underground dumptrucks and loaders. Along with Dart, Kenworth, Peterbilt and Foden it is now part of the PACCAR group making a variety of equipment including rear dumpers of 11 to 55 tons capacity, Teletram haulers for 15 to 25 tons, which unload by telescoping their bodies, and 1 to 13 cu yds loaders.

Shown is a 1963 telescoping low-profile truck from a range of similar 15, 24, 26 and 35-ton pivot-steer machines. They had 4 × 4 and Deutz V12, 290 bhp diesels. A self-loading version using the same motive unit was also made at the time by Sanford-Day as their Transloader.

RIGHT
Like the Joy, the Wakefield made by British Jeffery-Diamond was a self-loading dump-truck. The 1963 example shown had Leyland six-cylinder, 5.75 litre, 100 bhp diesel with two-range five-speed gearbox giving 10 gears both forwards and backwards, and a top speed of 33 mph. The machine had 4×4, dual controls and a struck capacity of $4\frac{1}{3}$ or 5 cu yds depending on whether SD55 or SD55R models. The loading shovel on both held 1 cu yd, had a lifting capacity of 3,600 lbs and a break-out force of 10,000 lbs. Payload was 17,000 lbs. The steering axle was mounted on a central pivot while the four-tyred 'back' axle was rigidly mounted.

CENTRE
As early as 1926 the New York firm of Walter Motor Truck Co patented a 4×4 tractor with rear dump semi-trailer and in the 1930s supplied rear and bottom dump outfits to various mining companies (see historical introduction). Then as now, Walters featured load-carrying sprung 'dead' axles with lockable differentials and drive shafts mounted above and separately from them. Drive was via jointed half-shafts to reduction gearing in the wheel rims, and there was a lockable third differential in the transfer case. The vehicle shown here was photographed in 1954 and has a 20 cu yd body for 20-ton loads (66,000 lbs gvw). It was outwardly similar to Walters of the 1930s to 1970s and could have Cummins six-cylinder, 743 cu ins, 200 bhp diesel or Waukesha six-cylinder, 1197 cu ins, 260 bhp gas engines. There were six forward and two reverse gears. From the 1960s onwards, nearly all Walter vehicles were crash tenders or else their longstanding speciality of 'Snow Fighters'.

BOTTOM
Werklust has made wheeled loading shovels in Holland since the late 1940s, adding six-wheel skip-moving trucks in 1974, followed by pivot-steer 6×6 dumptrucks.

Foden took a brief marketing interest in the latter before pulling out of the dumptruck field altogether. The recent WD3 shown has a Detroit six-cylinder 6.99-litre, 200 kW (273 bhp) diesel and Allison semi-automatic transmission with four ratios both forwards and backwards. There is drive to all three double reduction axles, or to just the front wheels in easier conditions. There are disc brakes and suspension is by rubber on the rear rocking beams with Dunlop Metalastik resilient bearings. Top speed is 45 km/h (28 mph) and payload is 30 tonnes in the 17.5m³ body. Overall length is 9.525m, width 2.75m and height 3.08m.

As well as SAVIEM and Berliet, France had another specialist heavy-truck maker building dumptrucks. It was Willème, whose TE 215 of the late 1950s is shown here. It carried a 15-tonne load and had a body of 7.5m³ struck capacity. The engine was Willème's own 13.54-litre, six-cylinder, 165 bhp diesel, and there was a three-range four-speed gearbox. The hub reduction rear axle was rigidly mounted and the undriven front one had semi-elliptic springs.

A version for hauling 10–13m³ semi-trailers was also offered with the same engine or with a straight-eight 18.05-litre 200/225 bhp diesel. The same engine options were also used in a 25-tonne rigid six-wheeler.

BELOW LEFT
One of the pioneers of tractor-based pivot-steer dumptrucks was the British firm of Whitlock, who started in the dumper business in 1955. The DD (Dinkum Dumper) 70, 85, and 95 came with 10-ton capacity, 7-8 cu yd bodies and 52 to 100 bhp Ford diesels. Then in 1963 they were joined by the DD105 shown here with 12 cu yd (heaped) body and Perkins 6.354 diesel. It had hydrostatic wheel motors giving a drawbar pull of up to 13,400 lbs.

BELOW RIGHT
After a commercially unsuccessful liaison with AEC for a few years from 1962, during which time many models used AEC diesels, Willème ceased production at the end of the 1960s, one of its last dumptrucks having a Volvo 275 bhp diesel. A licence to use the Willème name and some of its designs was acquired in 1971 by PRP, who made crane-carrier chassis.

The PRP-Willèmes included half-cab, forward control dumptrucks of up to 22 tonnes capacity on two axles with 7-litre, 240 bhp, six-cylinder Detroit diesels. The same engine was used in the 10-tonne (22-tonne gvw) TE 10 of the mid 1970s shown here. It had a ZF six-speed gearbox, semi-elliptic springs all round and planetary reduction drive axle.

The Willème name disappeared in 1979 when Creusot-Loire acquired PRP, and MOL adopted some of its designs. A very similar truck is now made by VPI.

An Index of Dumptruck Makers

Italic entries indicate illustrations